Illustrated Handbook

Museum of Fine Arts

Boston   1988

Library of Congress catalogue card no. 75-21769
ISBN 0-87846-092-6
Typeset in Linotype Optima by Thomas Todd Co., Boston, Massachusetts
Printed in U.S.A. by the Meriden-Stinehour Press, Meriden, Connecticut
Third Printing, 1988

This project was supported by a grant from the
National Endowment for the Arts, a federal agency

TABLE OF CONTENTS

INTRODUCTION

The Museum of Fine Arts, Boston, has outstanding collections of Chinese, Japanese, Indian, Mesopotamian, Egyptian, Greek, Roman, European, and American arts, including sculpture, paintings, prints, drawings, and decorative arts. The museum is managed by a board of trustees, including representatives of Harvard University, the Massachusetts Institute of Technology, the Boston Athenaeum, the city, and the state, acting through a professional staff. The museum was founded and has been carried on with the ideal of service to the community and with the conviction that art enriches life. It depends on the generosity of those who share this ideal and this conviction to make possible the active and varied program of special exhibitions and educational opportunities. The museum is reimbursed for a portion of the cost of its educational services to school children by the Commonwealth of Massachusetts, but its support comes almost entirely from private gifts. All gifts to the museum, whether of objects or money, are tax deductible. Names of givers are permanently attached to objects purchased with donated funds.

The Museum has two public entrances, Huntington Avenue and the West Wing. The building consists of three main floors. Each floor is divided into nine zones, and each zone is designated by a letter. Maps identifying specific spaces and collections within each gallery are available at the Information Center, West Wing. Please check maps.

FLOOR 1

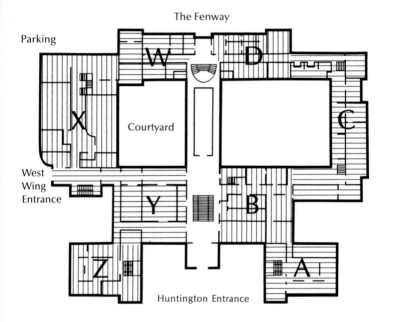

The Fenway

Parking

W

D

X

Courtyard

C

West
Wing
Entrance

Y

B

Z

A

Huntington Entrance

FLOOR 1

Zone W

American Painting

Zone X

Remis Auditorium
Museum Shop
Galleria Café
Riley Seminar Room
Foster Gallery
Rest Rooms

Zone Y

Asiatic Art
Islamic, Indian
Information Center
Members' Room
Torf Gallery

Zone Z

Asiatic Art
Japanese, Korean,
Southeast Asian

Zone A

Classical Art
Greek, Roman, Etruscan

Zone B

American Painting and Silver
Egyptian and Ancient Near Eastern Art
Musical Instruments Collection
Prints, Drawings, and Photographs

Zone C

American Decorative Arts
17th- to 19th-Century Period Rooms
Furniture and Silver
18th- and 19th-Century American Painting
Slide Library
Photographic Services

Zone D

American Painting

FLOOR 2

The Fenway

Huntington Avenue

FLOOR 2

Zone W

European Painting
Medieval
Renaissance
Baroque
18th-Century
Catalonian Chapel

Zone X

Gund Gallery
Fine Arts Restaurant
Rest Rooms

Zone Y

Asiatic Art
Chinese, Himalayan
European Painting

Zone Z

Asiatic Art
Chinese, Japanese

Zone A

Classical Art
Greek, Roman

Zone B

Egyptian Art
European Painting

Zone C

European Decorative Arts
English Tudor Room
French and English Period Rooms
Medieval Sculpture Galleries

Zone D

European Painting
17th- to 19th-Century
Impressionism

The Fenway

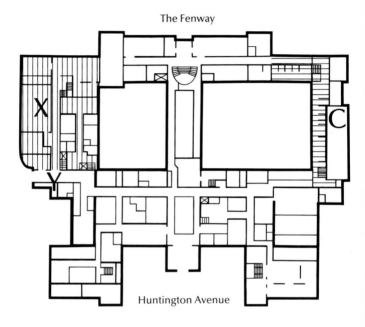

Huntington Avenue

FLOOR 0

Zone X

Education Services
Cafeteria
Workshop Studio
Rest Rooms
School Group Entrance

Zone Y

Staff Entrance

Zone C

American Decorative Arts
Period Rooms
Shaker Room
Ship Models

DEPARTMENT OF AMERICAN DECORATIVE ARTS AND SCULPTURE

As testimony to the creative imagination of artists and craftsmen who worked in this country, the collections of American decorative arts and sculpture range from the time of earliest permanent settlement to the present day. Except in sculpture, the greatest strength of the collections lies in pre-Civil War New England. Arts represented include furniture, silver, glass, pewter, ceramics, metalwares, and sculpture. There is also an important collection of ship models.

On FLOOR 1 (Fenway side) changing exhibits in the corridor-galleries display selected American decorative arts, paintings, prints, and textiles. Adjacent to this corridor are three rooms from Oak Hill, the home of Elizabeth (Derby) and Nathaniel West built in Peabody, Massachusetts, in 1801–1802. These rooms contain some of the original furnishings and several pieces made for Elizabeth's father, the wealthy Salem merchant Elias Hasket Derby.

Approached from the Huntington side of the museum, the American arts are introduced by a long corridor displaying silver made and used in this country from 1650 into the nineteenth century. The earliest major exhibitions of American silver took place at the Museum of Fine Arts in 1906 and 1911, and ever since those events the collection has grown in depth and quality: New England, New York, Philadelphia, Baltimore, Annapolis, and other

CHEST-ON-CHEST. John Cogswell (1738-1818). Mahogany. Boston, 1782. H. 97 in. *William Francis Warden Fund. 1973.289*
Considered by many the greatest piece of Boston furniture in the Chippendale style, this bombé or kettle-base chest-on-chest is signed and dated by its maker, "Made by John Cogswell in middle street Boston 1782." A masterpiece of eighteenth century American taste, skill, and craftsmanship, the chest-on-chest has a perfect unity of form and ornament. It was made for the family of the wealthy Salem merchant, Elias Hasket Derby.

centers are well represented. The incomparable strength of the collection is in Massachusetts silver — with no greater gathering of works by silversmith John Coney or the patriot-silversmith Paul Revere known elsewhere. Silver — both American and European — on loan from many churches in the Boston area, is also shown in this corridor. Main floor galleries focus on Queen Anne and Chippendale style furniture in the impressive M. and M. Karolik Collection of eighteenth century American arts, as well as an extensive display of neoclassical furniture of the early Republic.

On FLOOR 0 seventeenth century furniture, eighteenth century period rooms, a Shaker room, neoclassical sculpture, glass, ceramics, pewter, folk art, and ship models are on view, offering a broad sample of the quality and ingenuity of American craftsmanship and taste. The naive vigor of folk sculpture, the spiritual asceticism of Shaker design and the massive solidity of carved and painted seventeenth century furniture provide an interesting contrast with the seaport urbanity of the Jaffrey Room from Portsmouth, New Hampshire, or the products of America's first school of sculpture. Sculptors such as Thomas Crawford, Horatio Greenough, and others created a neoclassical ideal in chaste white marble, finding a devoted audience in Boston art patrons. Many of the statues have been in the museum's collection almost since they were made. A fine collection of bronze plaques by Augustus St. Gaudens documents Boston's literary elite at the end of the nineteenth century.

As the quality and importance of American decorative arts gain recognition, the museum collections will grow and change. The Department of American Decorative Arts and Sculpture, formed as a separate entity in 1971, is committed to the continuing improvement of the interpretation and scope of its collections.

WAINSCOT ARMCHAIR. Red oak. Massachusetts, Ipswich-Rowley area, 1680-1700. *Samuel Putnam Avery Fund. 37.316*

In wealthy seventeenth century households wainscot or "great" chairs such as this seated the head and the most important members of the family. Persons of lower station occupied backless stools and long benches, or "forms." With its straight back and rigid architectural framing of post and lintel construction, this armchair conveys the authority of its seventeenth century owner. The lower legs and the seat of the chair have been restored. In the seventeenth century a generous cushion would probably have been used for greater comfort.

TANKARD. Robert Sanderson (1609-1693). Silver. Boston, ca. 1670-1680.   H. 8¼
in. *Gift of John S. Ames and Mary Ames Frothingham. 37.263*
Robert Sanderson is the earliest American silversmith whose work is known. This
large tankard, with engraved flowers on the lid, was probably made for Isaac and
Mary (Balston) Vergoose, married in Boston about 1668, whose initials are on the
hinge plate.

SALVER. Timothy Dwight (1664-1692). Silver. Boston, ca. 1680.   D. 11¼ in.
Gift of Mr. and Mrs. Dudley Leavitt Pickman. 31.227
One of two pieces known by this silversmith, this salver is unique in its exotic
engraving of animals, vines, and flowers inspired by East Indian motifs. The
added initials are those of Thomas and Mary (Willoughby) Barton, who were
married in 1710, after the salver was made.

SUGAR BOX. John Coney (1655/6-1722). Silver. Boston, ca. 1680-90.   H. 4¾ in.
Gift of Mrs. Joseph Richmond Churchill. 13.421
This sugar box is one of the most intricate and elaborate pieces of early
American silver. Repoussé scrolls, panels, and bosses are combined to decorate
the oval box with hinged lid in a three-dimensional manner. In colonial times,
sugar and sweetmeats were such costly commodities that they were considered
worthy of extravagant display.

PRESS CUPBOARD. Attributed to Thomas Dennis (ca. 1640-1706). Oak and pine. Ipswich, Massachusetts, ca. 1680-90.   H. 61⅝ in. *Bequest of Charles Hitchcock Tyler. 32.251*
Considered a "status" piece, the press cupboard was probably the most elaborate and expensive piece of furniture in any seventeenth century American household. Decoratively carved and painted, with applied split turnings and bosses, its uses ranged from storage in the drawers and cupboards to display for silver, Delft, and valuables on the shelves and top.

STANDING SALT. Jeremiah Dummer (1645-1718). Silver. Boston, 1690-1700. H. 5½ in. *Bequest of Charles Hitchcock Tyler. 32.371*
Made by Boston's first native goldsmith, Jeremiah Dummer, this important standing salt is one of three known of American workmanship. Bands of reeding separate the octagonally shaped top and base from the circular body. The four scrolled knob finials probably supported a napkin or a dish as a cover for the precious salt inside.

PAIR OF CANDLESTICKS (one shown). John Noyes (1674-1749). Silver. Boston, ca. 1695-1700.   H. 9¼ in. *Gift of Miss Clara Bowdoin Winthrop. 54.594-595*
Seventeenth century American candlesticks are rare, and these survivors are extraordinarily handsome as well. With a boldness of mass, these important pieces have stop-fluted columnar stems, octagonal stepped bases, and bands of gadrooning. They are engraved with the Bowdoin family crest.

CHEST. Attributed to John Pease Jr. (1654-1734). Oak and pine. Enfield, Connecticut, ca. 1700-1714. H. 41½ in. *Bequest of Charles Hitchcock Tyler. 32.216*

The chest is carved in the intricate flat relief designs associated with the Hadley, Massachusetts, area. Stylized trailing vines, leaves, tulips, and geometric figures cover the front surface in both carved and painted decoration. The chest was presumably made for Mary Pease by her father John, a joiner, prior to her marriage in 1714.

HIGH CHEST ON FRAME. Japanned maple and pine. Boston, ca. 1725-1740.
H. 71¾ in. *Bequest of Charles Hitchcock Tyler. 32.227*
Made in the Queen Anne style with slender, graceful cabriole legs and high pad
feet, the high chest on frame is covered with a profusion of painted and gilded
decoration in the form of exotic birds and animals. The technique of japanning,
an attempt to imitate Oriental lacquer work, originated in England, and found
great favor among Boston cabinetmakers during the mid-eighteenth century.

DESK AND BOOKCASE. Walnut. Boston, ca. 1730.   H. 68½ in. *M. and M.*
Karolik Collection. 39.176
The small and compact proportions of this desk, together with the compass or
star inlay favored in Boston, mark this piece as a rarity in American furniture.
Its sculptural interior drawers introduce the block form which was more fully
developed in Boston and Newport later in the century. On the inside of the two
cabinet doors are specimens of penmanship done in 1766.

TEAKETTLE ON STAND. Jacob Hurd (1702/3-1758). Silver. Boston, ca. 1730-1740.
H. 14⅜ in. *Gift of Esther Lowell Abbott in memory of her mother, Esther Lowell*
Cunningham, granddaughter of James Russell Lowell. 1971.347a,b
Made by one of Boston's foremost silversmiths, this is the only published New
England teakettle from the colonial period. It was originally owned by the
Reverend John Lowell (1704–1767) in whose family it has descended. It is en-
graved with the coat of arms of Lowell quartering Leversedge.

ARMCHAIR. Walnut. Philadelphia, 1740-1750.   H. 41 in. *By exchange and C. H.*
Tyler Residuary Fund. 60.131
in Philadelphia the Queen Anne style was expressed by bold and symmetrically
balanced curves. Composed as pure sculptural form, the concave arm supports,
balloon seat, slipper feet, and scrolled splats combine here to achieve a total
harmony of design.

SIDE CHAIR. Mahogany. Newport, Rhode Island, ca. 1760.   H. 38½ in. *Edwin E. Jack Fund. 1971.280*
The precise outline and harmonious proportions of this Newport chair distinguish it from any other in the museum's collection. It has descended in a family, now living in Massachusetts, who by tradition trace it back to Joseph Vose (1738-1816), a colonel in Washington's army.

TEAPOT. Zachariah Brigden (1734-1787). Silver. Boston, ca. 1760.   H. 6 in. *Theodora Wilbour Fund in Memory of Charlotte Beebe Wilbour. 1971.50*
"The.Gift.of.Col¹: Epes. Sergeant. to. his./ daughter. Mary./ 1760." is engraved beneath the impaled Sargent-Winthrop coat of arms. The coat of arms is also found on Epes Sargent's bookplate and on a coffee pot made by Paul Revere II, both part of the museum's collection.

THE LIBERTY BOWL. Paul Revere II (1735-1818). Silver. Boston, 1768.   D. 11 in. *Gift by public subscription and from the Francis Bartlett Fund. 49.45*
The Liberty Bowl was made for fifteen members of the Sons of Liberty to commemorate the "glorious NINETY-TWO: Members/ of the Hon^bl House of Representatives of the Massachusetts-Bay." These heroic men defied George III by refusing to rescind a circular letter protesting against the English ministry and taxation without representation. Engraved with the names of the Sons of Liberty around the rim, the bowl is the most historic piece of American silver in existence.

BUREAU TABLE. Edmund Townsend (1736-1811). Mahogany. Newport, Rhode Island, ca. 1765-1775.   H. 33⅝ in. *M. and M. Karolik Collection. 41.579*
Also called a "kneehole chest of drawers," this superb example of Newport craftsmanship bears the original label of Edmund Townsend, a member of the Townsend-Goddard school of cabinetmakers. The bureau table was the first known work by Edmund Townsend to be discovered. It is of blockfront construction with applied convex shells.

TEA TABLE. Mahogany. Boston, ca. 1760-1780.   H. 27¾ in. *M. and M. Karolik Collection. 41.592*
This is one of but few surviving "turret-top" tables made in Boston before the Revolution. The fourteen turrets surrounding the edge of the table top have a molded edge designed to display teacups and saucers. The table is supported by four slender cabriole legs with carved acanthus leaves at the knees. Its raked-back claw and ball feet are characteristic of Boston craftsmanship.

COFFEE POT. Richard Humphreys (active 1771-1794). Silver. Philadelphia, ca. 1770-1780. H. 13½ in. *Gift in Memory of Dr. George Clymer by his wife, Mrs. Clymer. 56.589*
The superb rhythmic form of the coffee pot ranks it among the most beautiful examples of its kind. Its sculptural qualities are enhanced by elaborate swirling cast ornament at junctures of the spout and handle. It was undoubtedly made for a patron of wealth and position.

GOBLET. Paul Revere II (1735-1818). Silver, gilt lined. Boston, 1782. H. 5¼ in. *Pauline Revere Thayer Collection. 35.1769*
One of two known goblets of a set of six made for Nathaniel and Mary (Lee) Tracy by Revere, these handsome goblets are engraved and have spool-form stems and a high foot with gadrooned edge.

DESK AND BOOKCASE. George Bright (1726-1805). Mahogany. Boston, ca. 1780. H. 99½ in. *Bequest of Miss Charlotte Hazen. 56.1194*

Among the most robust works of eighteenth century American cabinetmaking, this desk and bookcase has a bombé-shaped base, a form most fully developed in Boston. It was made for the Boston merchant Samuel Barrett (1738-1798), who gave it to his daughter, Ann, upon her marriage in 1792. Elaborately carved and gilded ornament enriches the magnificent proportions and sculptural qualities of this desk.

SPEAKER'S DESK. John Shaw (1745-1829). Mahogany veneer on pine with satin-wood inlay. Annapolis, Maryland, ca. 1797.   H. 32¾ in. *Gift of Mr. and Mrs. Robert B. Choate. 63.12*

Inlaid with the Great Seal, the desk was made for use at the Maryland State House, probably in the House of Representatives. It is nearly identical to a labeled desk now standing in the Senate Chamber there.

CARD TABLE. Samuel McIntire (1757-1811). Mahogany and satinwood. Salem, ca. 1796. H. 30 in. *Gift of Miss Martha C. Codman, M. and M. Karolik Collection.* 23.16

Made for the Derby family of Salem, this card table, one of a pair, reflects the skill and craftsmanship of the master carver and architect Samuel McIntire. A full array of McIntire's favorite neoclassical motifs, including cornucopias, cascades of flowers, bows, baskets, and ovals, together with inlaid shell and fan-shaped rays, ornament the elegant table. Finishing the semicircular border of the table edge is a friezelike carved band found on other McIntire works.

CHEST-ON-CHEST. William Lemon (d. 1827) and Samuel McIntire (1757-1811). Mahogany. Salem, Massachusetts, ca. 1796. H. 102½ in. *M. and M. Karolik Collection.* 41.580

Considered the masterpiece of Salem Federal furniture, this double chest of drawers was made by William Lemon but carved by McIntire. It is thought to be the chest of drawers for which McIntire billed Elizabeth Derby, daughter of Elias Hasket Derby, in 1796. While the serpentine shape of the base and ogee bracket feet are reminiscent of mid-eighteenth century Chippendale form, the carved ornament with baskets of flowers, medallions, cornucopias, and putti super-impose the neoclassical tastes of the Federal period. A figure of Victory flanked by two carved urns crowns the top.

COVERED SUGAR BOWL. Attributed to the Mount Vernon Glass Works. Aquamarine glass. New York, ca. 1810-1840. H. 5½ in. *Edwin E. Jack Fund. 1971.276*
This sugar bowl, illustrated by George S. and Helen McKearin in *American Glass* (Crown Publishers, 1941, plate 122, no. 7), is a rare piece of pattern-molded glass, with a design of both horizontal and vertical ribbing. The Mount Vernon Glass Works is known to have produced glass of this aquamarine hue.

PITCHER. Ebenezer Moulton (1768-1824). Silver. Worked in Newburyport and Boston, 1811. H. 8¼ in. *Gift of the Heirs of Isaac Harris through Mrs. Edward Wyman. 13.560*
The raised barrel-form body with applied moldings and reeded bands is engraved "To M^r. ISAAC HARRIS/ For his intrepid and successful exertions/ on the roof of the Old South Church/ when on fire December 29^{nth} 1810/ the Society present this token of their/ GRATITUDE/ Boston January 29^{nth} 1811."

SIDEBOARD. Matthew Egerton (d. 1802). Mahogany and satinwood. New Jersey, ca. 1790-1800. H. 39¼ in. *M. and M. Karolik Collection. 39.141*
This six-legged sideboard with a bold serpentine front and crotch-grained veneer has the decorative quarter fans, bands of strings, and flowers found in furniture of the Federal period from the New York area. The sideboard, a new furniture form, achieved its first popularity at this time.

COMMODE. Thomas Seymour (1771-1843). Mahogany and satinwood. Boston, 1809. H. 41½ in. *Gift of Miss Martha C. Codman, M. and M. Karolik Collection. 23.19*
One of the most fully documented pieces of American furniture, this commode was made for Elizabeth Derby, carved by Thomas Whitman, and painted by John Ritto Penniman. George Hepplewhite's *The Cabinet-Maker and Upholsterer's Guide*, published in London in 1788, provided inspiration for the interesting semicircular form of this commode.

SIDE CHAIR. Samuel Gragg (active 1803-1837). Ash and hickory. Boston, ca. 1810-1820. H. 34⅛ in. *Charles Hitchcock Tyler Residuary Fund. 61.1074*
Of bentwood construction, this is perhaps the sleekest chair of its period made in America. It is completely painted in a muted white, with gold and sepia trim, and a colorful peacock feather on the central splat of the back. On the underside of the seat is the brand "S. Gragg/ Boston/ Patent."

CARD TABLE. Attributed to Duncan Phyfe (1768-1854). Mahogany. New York, ca. 1810-1820. H. 29½ in. *Francis Bartlett Fund. 58.19*
The very impressive supporting eagle was a favorite motif of carvers of the period of the New Republic. Duncan Phyfe, a cabinetmaker of great skill and creative ability, as well as a diligent worker and shrewd businessman, opened his New York furniture shop in 1792. At its peak, more than a hundred men were employed under Phyfe's personal supervision. Early productions were based on Thomas Seymour's *Drawing Book* designs, but Phyfe's furniture in the English Regency taste became so popular that his name is almost synonymous with this style in American furniture.

PIER TABLE. Emmons and Archbald (active 1813-1825). Mahogany and chestnut with mirror back and marble top. Boston, ca. 1813-1825. H. 32½ in. *Gift of the W. N. Banks Foundation. 1972.652*
American furniture in the Empire style, much in demand in the first half of the nineteenth century, reflected a widespread enthusiasm for France as the arbiter of taste. The imposing appearance of the table is emphasized by the architectural solidity of the marble top, pillar and pilaster supports, and a heavy shelf base. Color is as important as form to the effect of Empire pier tables, and this one, one of a pair thought to be the only pair of labeled American pier tables extant, is richly ornamented with highly figured veneers, and ormolu mounts, caps, and bases in classical motifs.

HEBE AND GANYMEDE. Thomas Crawford (1813-1857). Marble. Rome, 1842.
H. 68½ in. *Gift of Charles C. Perkins. 76.702*
One of the first museum accessions, *Hebe and Ganymede* is signed and dated
1842, the year the sculptor completed the plaster model in Rome from which
the finished marble is derived. Based on a Greek myth, the work imparts an
aura of quiet and a sense of calm, deep thought.

CASTOR AND POLLUX. Horatio Greenough (1805-1852). Marble with gilded
walnut base. Florence, 1847-1851.   H. 34½ in. *Bequest of Mrs. Horatio
Greenough. 92.2642*
The sculptor's understanding of the antique and the ideals of the neoclassical
period can be seen in the oval bas-relief plaque carved during his last years in
Florence. According to mythology, the brothers Castor and Pollux dwelt alter-
nately in Hades and heaven. Greenough depicts them as they pass each other
en route.

THE FURY. Edward R. Thaxter (1854-1881). Marble. Naples, ca. 1881. H. 26 in.
William E. Nickerson Fund. 63.5
This emotionally expressive face, carved with intense realism, is signed "E. R.
Thaxter." In a period when aesthetic conventions were strongly directed against
the baroque, it is remarkable that Thaxter achieved such dramatic modeling of
form. His work reveals a deep understanding for Bernini and other related
Neapolitan sculptors. This bust, acquired by the museum as *The Fury*, probably
portrays Meg Merrilies, a half-crazed sibyl who was a prominent character in
Sir Walter Scott's novel *Guy Mannering*.

THE FLYING CLOUD. H. E. Boucher. Wood, cloth, and glass. New York, ca. 1915.
H. 31 in. *Gift of Frederick C. Fletcher. 35.42*
The clipper ship *Flying Cloud* was built by Donald McKay in 1851 at his East
Boston shipyard. This scale model by H. E. Boucher was made from the original
plans and data and executed in exacting detail. The *Flying Cloud* was one of
the handsomest clippers afloat, with cabins finished in rosewood and mahogany.
She was a large vessel, but fast enough to claim two record passages from New
York to San Francisco in eighty-nine days — records never beaten under sail.

DEPARTMENT OF ASIATIC ART

In Asiatic art the Boston Museum is preeminent. Its Asiatic collections are unrivaled in the Western world for the number, variety, and importance of the masterpieces they contain. They are also so extensive, so representative of the manifold phases and media of Asian art that they constitute the largest assemblage to be found anywhere under one roof, and hence offer a matchless opportunity for studying the artistic expression of all the peoples of Asia.

The artistic traditions included within the scope of the department fall into three major cultural units. The Far Eastern tradition is that of China, Japan, and Korea, but it extends westward as well into the vast areas of Central Asia. The culture of Islam includes the whole of the Middle East, yet also stretches out to North Africa and spreads eastward to India with a further leap into Southeast Asia. The third complex of cultures is that of the subcontinent of India. Under the impetus of Hindu and Buddhist religions its artistic influence reaches northward through Nepal and Tibet and southward through Sri Lanka, Java, Burma, Thailand, and Cambodia. Especially strong are the collections of objects from the Far East, from India, and from Iran.

The range in time covered by collections in the department is comparable to the range in geography. The earliest pieces, finds from the Indus Valley where the museum made an important excavation in 1935-36, date back to the third millennium B.C., while the most recent are contemporary woodblock prints from Japan.

The variety of techniques represented is equally rich. The arts of China and Japan begin with ceramics of the Neolithic Age. In China the succeeding Bronze Age produced metal shapes distinguished in form, extraordinarily perfect in casting, and unique in decoration. Other high points in the history of artistry can be seen in silver-inlaid bronzes from medieval Persia, as well as with the sword and its furnishings from Japan.

Monumental sculpture ranging in style from the geometric through the anthropomorphic to culminate in more baroque tendencies is represented by noble examples from India, China, and Japan. The art of painting in the Far East, where a uniquely pliant brush and specially sized background permit a development of this art impossible in the West, can be traced in China from the first century B.C. onward, with other styles emerging in Japan and Korea. Using a different brush the painters of Persia and India have created forms expressive of their cultures in the firmness of lines and the richness of colors.

Outstanding examples of calligraphy from both the Far and the Near East show the Oriental's respect for the mystery of writing, in ages when knowledge was the privilege of a few. On the other hand, the color prints of Japan, where the museum's collection is probably the most extensive in the world, are the taste of commoners in a feudal society, and have no parallel in the West until modern times.

These are but a few of the media represented in the museum's Oriental collections. Mention should at least be made of the richness of the collections also in textiles, lacquer, and ceramics. And finally it must be pointed out that any selection of fifty objects from an array of treasures dating from the dawn of civilization and coming from every part of Asia can only suggest the importance and distinction of the collection as a whole.

This great assemblage owes its existence to gifts and bequests. Chief among them are: the William Sturgis Bigelow Collection of Japanese art of all varieties (some 60,000 objects in all) and the Fenollosa-Weld Collection of Japanese paintings, both acquired in Japan during the 1880's; the Denman Waldo Ross Collection, comprising varied types of Far Eastern and Indian art; the Charles B. Hoyt Collection, mainly of Chinese and Korean ceramics; and the William S. and John T. Spaulding Collection of Japanese prints. These important collections, continually supplemented by numerous individual gifts and bequests as well as by frequent purchases, account for the Boston Museum's unequalled holdings in the arts of Asia. Further growth has been encouraged through legacies from Mrs. John G. Coolidge, Marshall H. Gould, Charles B. Hoyt, Frederick L. Jack, Keith McLeod, and other generous friends of the department.

Few catalogues of the collections are available. Miss Chie Hirano's *Kiyonaga, a Study of His Life and Works* is far more than the first monograph written about a Japanese print artist, for it relates his work to the whole of the eighteenth century. The *Catalogue of the Morse Collection of Japanese Pottery*, which appeared in 1901, is still the only major work of its kind in English. The second *Portfolio of Chinese Paintings*, covering the Yüan to Ch'ing periods by Kojiro Tomita and Hsien-chi Tseng, completes the record of the collection in this field. A catalogue of the Charles B. Hoyt Collection will be published in three volumes, two of which have already appeared. The third volume, mainly on Korean ceramics, is in preparation. A selection from the masterpieces of the collection is shown in *Museum of Fine Arts Boston: Oriental Art* (1969).

THE FIVE-COLORED PARAKEET (detail). By the Emperor Hui-tsung (reigned, A.D. 1101-1125). Handscroll, ink and colors on silk. China, Northern Sung period. 53.3 x 125.1 cm. *Maria Antoinette Evans Fund.* 33.364

This "tall" scroll, as the Chinese call it, is one of the finest of the works considered by authorities to be definitely by the emperor Hui-tsung. The scroll displays not only the emperor's outstanding painting but also his much admired calligraphy, known as the "slender gold script." Both the painting and the calligraphy commemorate a five-colored parakeet that had been brought to the emperor's garden of apricot blossoms from the south. Between the ten lines of writing and the charming live study of the exotic bird and flowers is Hui-tsung's signature and seal. Though partly damaged, this rare and important signature can still be read as: "Composed, written, and painted by the emperor."

MONGOLIAN YOUTH. Bronze with two birds in jade. China, Warring-States period, ca. early fourth century B.C.   H. 28.5 cm. *Maria Antoinette Evans Fund. 31.976*

This superb example of early Chinese bronze sculpture shows a young person intently gazing at two jade doves chained to the top of two bronze sticks modeled in the shape of branches. The figure reveals many interesting details of the dress and hair style of the period and is therefore not only a fascinating work of art but also an important source of evidence for early cultural history in China. The figure is said to have been found at Chin-ts'un, north of Lo-yang, the ancient capital of the Eastern Chou dynasty. Recent archaeological finds from China seem to confirm this site as the origin of the statue. If this work was indeed produced in the very center of China, it is interesting that it should have such a non-Chinese appearance. For example, the braided hair and the left-folded dress of the youth contrast with the Chinese custom of the time. However, these attributes correspond to the Chinese descriptions of the nomads who had lived in the northern steppes since the time of Confucius. It is quite likely, therefore, that this work represents the extent to which the Chinese knew their northern neighbors in the fourth century B.C.

STONE SLAB FROM THE TOMB OF A CENTRAL ASIAN OR SASANIAN MER-
CHANT. China, Northern Ch'i period (A.D. 550-577).   46.8 x 113 cm. *Gift of
Denman Waldo Ross and G. M. Lane. 12.588*
One of a pair, this stone slab was once part of a funerary monument for a
Central Asian or Sasanian resident of China. During the second half of the sixth
century Chinese taste for the foreign and exotic exerted its influence on the
arts for the first time. Although the execution is typically Chinese, the personages and customs illustrated on this minutely carved relief are all from the
country of origin of the deceased.

RITUAL VESSEL OF DUKE HSI OF THE STATE OF LU. Bronze tripod, *Li* type.
China, early Western Chou period, inscription datable to early 10th century B.C.
H. 17 cm. (from handle to foot). Diam. 14.6 cm. *Grace M. Edwards Fund. 47.230*
Among numerous Chinese bronze vessels of the period now preserved inside
and outside China, this *Li* tripod is considered unique and important for two
reasons. First, the thirteen-character inscription engraved under the rim inside
the wall of the tripod has provided one of the most helpful documents in
establishing the chronology of the early Western Chou dynasty, which moved
eastward and conquered the Shang dynasty in 1027 B.C. According to Ch'en
Meng-chia of the Institute of Archaeology, Peking, the Duke Hsi reigned in the
State of Lu, today's Western Shantung Province, between 994 and 989 B.C. On
the basis of the duke's regnal dates, the Boston *Li* tripod can be assigned to the
very early part of the Western Chou dynasty. Secondly, the structure of the
t'ao-t'ieh (monster mask) decorating the exterior of the *Li* shows a distinct
change from its predecessors of the late Shang period. Several unusual motifs
adopted in the decor are little known prior to or after this period. For example,
the stylized nose of the *t'ao-t'ieh* is decorated with four eyes, two on either
side of the central flange. Also each of the three *t'ao-t'ieh* masks is bounded
by two decorative bands terminating in three claws, a motif found on no other
Chinese bronze vessels.

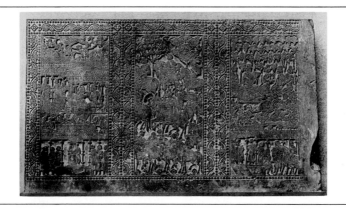

BODHISATTVA, FROM THE WHITE HORSE MONASTERY, LO-YANG. Limestone.
China, Northern Wei dynasty, ca. A.D. 530.   H. 196.5 cm. *Gift of Denman Waldo
Ross in memory of Okakura Kakuzo. 13.2804*
One of the largest pieces of stone sculpture ever to come out of China, this
finely carved figure shows a close resemblance to the statuary of the cave
temple complex of Lung-men, especially that in cave XXIV, which can be dated
by an inscription to A.D. 527. The cuspidate necklace is identical with those of
the figures in this cave, but the softly flowing folds of the drapery suggest a
slightly later date, perhaps during the early years of the Eastern Wei period. The
details of the back are summarily indicated, suggesting that the figure was not
originally part of a cave temple but one of the earliest Buddhist freestanding
figures from China. In the spring of 1903 the Japanese painter and amateur
archaeologist Hayasaki Kōkichi witnessed the excavation of this statue from the
central courtyard of the Pai-ma-ssu (White Horse Monastery) near Lo-yang.
Although he and his step-uncle, Okakura, tried repeatedly to acquire this
masterpiece for the museum, the sculpture disappeared from the temple, to
reappear in Paris shortly before Okakura's death.

A DVĀRAPĀLA (gateway guardian). Dry lacquer. China, Sung dynasty, 10th-11th century. H. 58 cm., w. 26 cm. *Hoyt Collection. 50.1073*
The tradition of making statues in the dry lacquer technique, hollow and light, perhaps for processional use, must have existed from a much earlier period in China. Many life-sized eighth century sculptures exist in Japan. Examples from China are exceptionally rare.

HORSE. Pottery, glazed. China, T'ang dynasty (618-906). H. 76 cm., diam. 79.6 cm. *John Gardner Coolidge Collection. 46.478*
According to T'ang sumptuary laws, the number and size of ceramic mortuary gifts, vessels as well as figurines, placed in tombs depended upon the rank and status of the deceased. Large figurines such as this horse usually come from the tombs of noblemen or high military officials.

ALTARPIECE WITH AMITABHA AND ATTENDANTS. Bronze. China, Sui dynasty, dated in accordance with A.D. 593. H. 76.5 cm. *Gift of Mrs. W. Scott Fitz (22.407) and gift of Edward Jackson Holmes in memory of his mother, Mrs. W. Scott Fitz (47.1407-1412)*
This elaborate representation of Amitabha's Western Paradise is a masterpiece of bronze casting of the Sui period. The principal figure is the Buddha Amitabha, seated on a reticulated lotus throne. Above it is a flowering tree over which hover the Seven Buddhas of the Past and around which apsaras (heavenly nymphs) fly. On each side stand three figures: a figure with a coiled headdress (a so-called Pratyeka Buddha), a disciple of the Buddha, and a Bodhisattva. These figures are all detachable, as are the two Guardian Kings, the two lions, and the incense burner, on the front of the dais. When the altar was excavated in Hopei Province about seventy-five years ago, the figures on the front of the dais were removed and sold before the altarpiece came into the possession of the Viceroy Tuan Fang. They were reunited with the altar only after it had been in Boston twenty-five years.

VASE. Pottery. Tz'ŭ-chou ware. China, Sung dynasty, 11th-12th century. H. 39.1 cm., diam. 19.6 cm. *Hoyt Collection. 50.1058*

TARTARS TRAVELING ON HORSEBACK (detail). Attributed to Li Tsan-hua (ca. 900-937). Full color on silk. China, Five Dynasties. 27.8 x 12.51 cm. *Keith Mc-Leod Fund. 52.1380*

THE THIRTEEN EMPERORS (section). Traditionally attributed to Yen Li-pen (died A.D. 673). Handscroll, ink and colors on silk. China, second half of the seventh century, T'ang period (second section); ca. 11th century replacement. 51 x 551 cm. *Denman Waldo Ross Collection. 31.643*

Despite the deterioration that has occurred over the centuries, this fragile scroll is nevertheless of unique importance for the light it sheds on Chinese figure painting of the seventh century. Thirteen groups of figures are depicted, each with an idealized portrait of an emperor and court attendants. The accompanying inscriptions identify the emperors, who are depicted according to a chronological (but not sequential) order, beginning with the fourth emperor of the Western Han period, Wen-ti (reign 179-163 B.C.) and concluding with the second emperor of the Sui period, Yang-ti (reign 605-617 A.D.). The criteria used in selecting the imperial personages represented here are unclear, for not all of them were of major historical importance. Subtle differences indicate that the first section of the scroll, with the six earlier emperors, was not executed at the same time as the last section, with its representations of seven later monarchs: not only are the silk grounds different in weave but the ink and pigments also vary. Furthermore, there are small but significant variations in the details of the brushwork that indicate that the two sections were executed by different hands. It is believed that the second section is a genuine work of the second half of the seventh century, while the first section is a careful copy, probably executed about the eleventh century during the Northern Sung dynasty and substituted for the original portion at that time. The scroll has traditionally been identified with the name of Yen Li-pen, the great innovative figure painter of the seventh century. Although conclusive evidence to support this traditional attribution is lacking, there is nothing in the style and details of the painting that contradicts the possibility of a seventh century date.

LADIES PREPARING NEWLY WOVEN SILK (detail). By the emperor Hui-tsung (1082-1135) after a work by Chang Hsüan, a court painter active about 713-742. Full color on silk. China, Sung dynasty. 37 x 143.5 cm. *Chinese and Japanese Special Fund. 12.886*
Though the emperor Hui-tsung copied a work of the eighth century, the absence of background, the restrained poise of the figure composition, and the variety of strong colors, doubtless all preserve characteristics of the painting of the T'ang dynasty.

THE LOHANS FEEDING A HUNGRY SPIRIT. By Lin T'ing-kuei, dated in accordance with A.D. 1178. Hanging scroll mounted as a panel, ink, gold, and colors on silk. China, Southern Sung period. 111.5 x 53.1 cm. *Denman Waldo Ross Collection. 06.292*
This painting, together with nine others in the museum's collection, was originally part of a set of one hundred paintings representing the Five Hundred Lohans (*Arhats* in Sanskrit, the disciples and followers of Śākyamuni Buddha). These works were originally dedicated in the temple of Hui-an-ssu near Ning-po, Chekiang province. Several scrolls, including the two pieces in the museum's collection, bear dedicatory inscriptions written in gold by the Priest I-shao of the temple. The inscriptions indicate that the set was made around 1178 either by Lin T'ing-kuei or by Chou Chi-ch'ang, both of whom probably were local professional artists. The inscription by I-shao on this painting gives the date as the eighth moon of the year 1178, but no artist's name is mentioned. Judging from its style and composition, we nevertheless can clearly identify the painting as a work by Lin T'ing-kuei. This set of Lohan paintings was brought to Japan by Japanese monks who had gone to China to study Buddhism in the thirteenth century. The paintings came to play an important role in the iconographical evolution of Japanese paintings representing Lohan (Japanese: *Rakan*). As early as 1386 this set had already been copied by the famous Japanese monk-painter Minchō (1352-1431), whose copies are now preserved in the Tōfukuji temple in Kyoto. Because of the reliability of their attribution, these religious figure paintings have become a very important source for the study of Chinese figure painting of the twelfth and thirteen centuries.

THE NINE DRAGONS (detail). By Ch'en Jung, dated in accordance with 1244. Handscroll, ink, and touches of red on paper. China, Southern Sung period. 46.3 x 1096.4 cm. *Francis Gardner Curtis Furd. 17.1697* In an extraordinary display of powerful and versatile brushwork, the artist Ch'en Jung has painted nine dragons of different types and in varying poses, frolicking among clouds and waves. Contrary to the dragon image in Christianity, the Chinese view their dragon as rather innocent and possessing a variety of virtues. Of all the Chinese paintings of dragons in existence today, this scroll is remarkable for its artistry as well as for its expression of the everlasting affection of the Chinese toward the dragon. The artist, who was famous for this genre, added two inscriptions in very individual handwriting to accompany the dragons. The date of the painting, in accordance with A.D. 1244, is given in one of the two inscriptions.

THE BODHISATTVA AVALOKITEŚVARA (KUAN-YIN). Wood. China, Sung dynasty. 12th century.   H. 14.1 cm., w. 88 cm. *Harvey Edward Wetzel Fund. 20.590* The compassionate Bodhisattva Kuan-yin (Sanskrit: *Avalokiteśvara*) is represented in the Posture of Royal Relaxation (Sanskrit: *Mahārājīlā*), the right arm supported by the raised right knee, the left leg hanging down and the head slightly inclined. During the reign of the Sung dynasty and that of its successor in the North, the Chin, this type of wooden sculpture became common in the northern parts of China, especially in the province of Shansi. During restoration a thick layer of overpainting was removed from the image, revealing bright colors as well as *kirigane* (cut gold foil) designs underneath. As a result, the original resplendent quality of the image is now again apparent. Images of this type were commonly placed in front of brightly colored wall paintings representing the legendary abode of Avalokiteśvara at Potalaka.

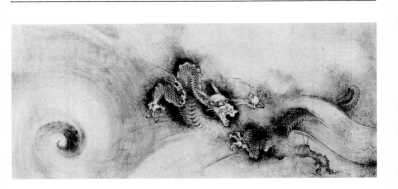

ENJOYING THE MID-AUTUMN MOON. By Shen Chou (1427-1509). Handscroll, ink and light color on paper. China, Ming period, datable to A.D. 1468. 30.4 x 134.5 cm. *Chinese and Japanese Special Fund. 15.898*

Shen Chou was the most important painter of the Ming period (1368-1644). With his deep understanding and synthesis of literati (*Wen Jen*) painting styles developed in the fourteenth century he influenced countless later artists of the literati school. The Boston scroll is a good representative of the work of Shen Chou. It consists of a simple landscape with scholars viewing the full autumn moon and two poems composed and elegantly written by the master. The artist intended the beauty of the landscape to be enhanced by and dependent on the content of the poems as well as the calligraphical style. The combination of painting, poem, and calligraphy into an "aesthetic trinity" was considered the highest form of artistic expression by painters of the literati school.

LOTUS. By Chu Ta, also known as Pa-ta-shan-jen (1626-after 1705). Ink on paper. China, Ch'ing dynasty. 185 x 89.8 cm. *Keith McLeod Fund. 56.495*

HANIWA (terracotta mortuary figure). Japan, Proto-historic period, fifth-sixth century A.D. H. 590 cm., diam. 246 cm. *Edward S. Morse Fund. 62.356*

This provocative figure of a young girl holding a cup is typical of the *haniwa* (lit.: "clay cylinders"), the striking statuary that was set up in large numbers on and around the burial tumuli of Japanese nobles, a practice that reached its height during the fourth and fifth centuries.

TEBAKO ("handy box"). Lacquer with gold decor. Japan, Kamakura period, late 13th-early 14th century. 15.5 x 23.5 x 31 cm. *Martha Silsbee Fund. 31.1*

This superb example of early Japanese lacquer has pewter rims and is fitted with two brass ring-holders in the shape of butterflies. The cover decoration consists of a weeping willow and a flowering plum with birds flying above, while designs of autumnal flowers cover the sides. Three of the rocks at the base of the trees on the cover have characters that, when combined, read *Cho sei den*, a reference to a palace hall built for the T'ang emperor Hsüan-tsung, the "Hall of Longevity." The term, which passed on in Japanese literature, has a felicitous connotation and appears on several other lacquer boxes of the Kamakura period.

THE ADVENTURES OF KIBI-DAIJIN IN CHINA. Handscroll. Japan, Heian period, late 12th century. H. 32.2 cm., l. 2442 cm. *William Sturgis Bigelow Collection by exchange. 32.131*
This famous handscroll illustrates the legendary adventures of a Japanese ambassador to the Chinese court, Kibi no Makibi, during his mission to T'ang China in 753. The haughty Chinese subject Kibi to a series of tests designed to embarrass him, but his erudition and resourcefulness are such that he invariably defeats his hosts at their own game. He is aided in these contests by the ghost of the celebrated poet Abeno Nakamaro, who appears here as a red, demon-like figure. Because of its great length the scroll has been divided into four sections. It is among the finest Yamato-e paintings outside of Japan.

THE BODHISATTVA MAITREYA (Japanese: *Miroku-bosatsu*). By Kaikei. Wood, gilt. Japan, Kamakura period, dated 1189. H. 1.07 cm. *Chinese and Japanese Special Fund. 20.723*
This superb specimen of late twelfth century Japanese sculpture, executed in the *yosegi* ("joined blocks") manner, was probably originally installed in the Kōfukuji, a temple in Nara. It represents the Bodhisattva Maitreya, the Buddha of the Future. It came into the hands of Okakura Kakuzo, who served for some years as curator of the Asiatic Department, in 1903-1904. Several years later, when it was repaired, a sūtra scroll was found inside with a colophon indicating that the piece was executed by the master Kaikei in 1189. It is the earliest known dated work by this celebrated Buddhist monk-sculptor.

THE HORSE-HEADED KANNON (Japanese: *Batō-Kannon*). Ink, colors, and gold on silk. Japan, Heian period, 12th century. H. 165.5 cm., w. 83 cm. *Fenollosa-Weld Collection. 11.4035*
Batō Kannon (Sanskrit: *Hayagrīva*), one of the Esoteric manifestations of the Bodhisattva Avalokiteśvara (Japanese: *Kannon*), is represented here with three heads and eight arms, seated on an elaborately decorated lotus throne against a halo of golden floral decor. Originally the image was probably one of a set of six Kannon representations, each conceived as a saviour of one of the Six States of Transmigration. Above the crown designating the Bodhisattva rank rises a small figure of a horse's head symbolic of the deity's role as a saviour of the animal world.

THE BURNING OF THE SANJŌ PALACE (detail). Handscroll. Japan, Kamakura period, 13th century.   H. 41.3 cm., l. 699.7 cm. *Fenollosa-Weld Collection. 11.4000*

On the night of January 19, 1160, the Sanjō Palace, residence of the retired emperor Go-Shirakawa, was attacked by a combined force led by Fujiwara Nobuyori and Minamoto Yoshitomo. The palace was set to the torch, many attendants slaughtered, and the emperor abducted. These events portrayed here are part of the literary chronicle known as the *Heiji-monogatari,* which describes the battles for supremacy between two powerful clans, the Taira and the Minamoto. Originally this extensive chronicle was portrayed in a large series of handscrolls, but today only three of the scrolls and a few fragments are preserved. This famous scroll is the finest of the extant examples.

LANDSCAPE. By Bunsei. Hanging scroll. Ashikaga period, ca. mid-15th century. H. 73 cm., w. 33 cm. *Special Chinese and Japanese Fund. 05.203*

Although only a few authentic paintings from the hand of the master Bunsei are extant today, these pieces nevertheless provide clear evidence that he was one of the most gifted artists active during the mid-fifteenth century in Japan. Although his biography is unclear, the fact that two portraits of Zen priests (one a mid-fifteenth century contemporary) by Bunsei are still preserved in the Daitokuji, the renowned Zen temple in Kyoto, suggests that he may have been a priest attached to that temple. Bunsei's stylistic indebtedness to the influential master Shubun (active early mid-fifteenth century) is apparent here, but it has been suggested that Bunsei's landscape paintings also show the influence of Korean monochrome landscape painting of the period.

MONKEYS AND BIRDS IN TREES. By Sesshū (1420-1506). Six-panel screen (one of a pair). Japan, Ashikaga period, dated 1491.   H. 160.6 cm., w. 61 cm. (each panel). *Fenollosa-Weld Collection. 11.4141*
Sesshū is among the greatest of the fifteenth century Japanese Zen priest-painters and probably the best known. Indebted in a general way to Chinese ink painting of the Sung period, his most characteristic works nevertheless stand apart from the earlier Chinese tradition and have a distinct Japanese flavor in their conception and brushwork. Monkeys were a popular subject in Japanese monochrome painting, and this representation was executed, according to the inscription in the upper right corner, when the artist was (by Japanese reckoning) seventy-two years of age.

THE CHINESE SAGES PO I AND SHU CH'I. By Kano Naonobu. Six-panel folding screen (one of a pair), Japan, Edo period.   H. 1488 cm., w. (each panel) 602 cm. *Fenollosa-Weld Collection. 11.4281*
This screen with its breadth of conception and bold brushwork is characteristic of the style of the talented master of the Kano school, Naonobu (1607-1650). Subjects with moral or ethical overtones, generally drawn from ancient Chinese literature, were often depicted by members of the Kano school. Here, two brothers, Po I and Shu Ch'i, talk in mountain solitude. Their father had wished Shu Ch'i, the younger brother, to succeed him. But Shu Ch'i did not think it right thus to dispossess his elder brother. Po I, on the other hand, could not disobey his father's desire in regard to the succession. To solve this moral dilemma, the brothers decided to go into exile together.

MATSUSHIMA. By Ogata Kōrin. Six-panel folding screen. Japan, Edo period, early 18th century.   H. 155 cm., w. (each panel) 63 cm. *Fenollosa-Weld Collection. 11.4584*
In this dynamic composition probably inspired by Sōtatsu's earlier rendition of the same theme (Freer Gallery of Art, Washington, D.C.), Korin (1658-1716) has skillfully depicted the famous landscape of pine-clad islands and turbulent waves in the Bay of Matsushima, northeast of Sendai. The almost eight hundred islands constitute one of the Three Famous Views of Japan, and were painted frequently by members of Kōrin's school. This screen was one of the pieces obtained by Ernest Fenollosa on his first trip to Kyoto in 1880. It may well be the first major work of Japanese art to be acquired by a foreigner.

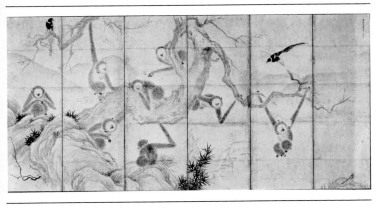

THE BUDDHA BHAIṢAJYAGURU (YAKSA YORAE). Gilt bronze. Korea, Silla dynasty, ca. eighth century. H. 36 cm. *Gift of Edward Jackson Holmes in memory of his mother, Mrs. W. Scott Fitz. 32.436*
This elegant statue of Yaksa Yorae, the Medicine Buddha (Sanskrit: *Bhaiṣajyaguru*) exemplifies the Korean adaptation of the Chinese T'ang style in its most classic form. The fine details of the elaborate lotus stand and the balanced proportions of the standing figure are typical of the metal sculpture of the Silla dynasty of the eighth century. It antedates the period during which a more ponderous style of figures with disproportionately large heads began to prevail. For many years this statue, the finest piece of Korean sculpture in the museum's collection, belonged to Okakura Kakuzo (1862-1913), the distinguished Japanese art historian who expanded the museum's activities from Japan into the Asian mainland.

EWER AND BASIN. Silver gilt. Korea, Koryŏ period, 11th-12th century. Ewer: h. 33 cm.; basin: h. 17 cm. *George Nixon Black Fund. 35.646*
The scalloped body, the spout, and the handle of the ewer all have shapes inspired by bamboo forms. The cover consists of three conventional lotuses, surmounted by a phoenix. The ewer fits into a basin of similarly scalloped shape; both vessels are engraved with a decoration of floral sprays. Their shapes resemble those of ceramic types from Korea as well as from Northern Sung China.

VASE. Celadon with black and white inlays. Korea, Koryŏ period, 12th century. H. 31 cm. *Hoyt Collection. 50.989*
The vase is of the so-called *mae-byong* type, derived from Northern Sung Chinese prototypes. It is decorated with a simple design of cranes and wind-blown bamboos, executed in inlaid white and black slip. The utter simplicity of the design suggests that this vase is one of the relatively early examples of inlaid celadon, made not long after this typically Korean technique was first developed and perfected.

Indian, Southeast Asian, and Islamic Art

LARGE PAINTED JAR. Chanhu-daro, Sind, Pakistan. Harappa culture, ca. 3000 B.C. 1.39 cm. *Chanhu-daro Expedition. 36.2917*

HEAD OF A DEVATĀ. Stucco. Afghanistan, Hadda, 5th century A.D.   H. 17 cm., w. 15.4 cm. *Denman Waldo Ross Collection. 31.191*

YAKṢĪ TORSO. Sandstone. India, Sanchi, first century B.C.   H. 72 cm. *Denman Waldo Ross Collection. 29.999*

The sculpture of a tree-dwelling dryad originally served as a bracket figure on the gateway of the great Buddhist *stūpa* at Sanchi. Like the slightly earlier *stūpa* at Bharhut, this monument was surrounded by a stone railing, but here the railing was left without decoration, which was instead profusely applied to the four entrance gates. This sculpture in all probability came from the southern gate, which seems to have been the first to be completed. Whereas the *stūpa*, the traditional Buddhist commemorative monument built over the ashes or other relics of a saint, was of monumental simplicity, the gates were decorated with stories from the life of the Buddha or from his previous births with animals and with these tree-dryads, who, by merely touching the branch of a tree, could bring it to blossom and bear fruit. The figure exemplifies for the first time the Indian artist's mastery of the technique of rendering in three-dimensional sculpture the sensuous feminine beauty of such symbols of fertility.

UMĀ-MAHEŚVARA. Gilt copper. Nepal, 13th century.   H. 24.8 cm. *Marshall H. Gould and Frederick L. Jack Funds. 68.3*
The great god Śiva and his wife Umā sit in a posture of relaxation on a lotus throne placed on a rectangular dais surrounded by their children and attendants. Representations of this divine couple known as Uma-Mahesvara were quite popular in Nepal, where they were executed in stone as well as in bronze. This piece is one of the most elaborate examples of this type.

CELESTIAL DANCER. Bronze. Cambodia, Khmer, late 12th-early 13th century. H. 39.3 cm. *Ross-Coomaraswamy Collection. 22.686*
The figure is standing in a graceful dancing pose on a lotus-like flower, springing from a flowering spray that terminates in a half-opened bud revealing a similar but smaller female figurine. She raises both hands, touching a flame-fringed trifoliate arch, the lower corners of which terminate in *nāga* (snake) heads. This superb example of Khmer bronze casting from Cambodia probably was once part of a lamp or standard. Rows of celestial dancers executed in stone relief occur on several of the great monuments of Khmer architecture.

ASIATIC ART | 61

THE HOUR OF COWDUST. India, Kāṅgrā, late 18th century. 0.216 x 270 m.
Ross-Coomaraswamy Collection. 22.683
Religious narration, where Kṛṣṇa leads home a herd of cattle, and genre setting,
a keenly observed scene of village life, unite to present the basic point of view
of Hindu painting.

POET SEATED IN A GARDEN. India, Deccan, ca. A.D. 1610. 12.2 x 10.3 cm.
Goloubew Collection, Francis Bartlett Donation of 1912 and Picture Fund. 14.663
The poet is seated in a garden, books, inkstand, and flask in front of him. The
signature on the back is that of the famous calligrapher Mir 'Imad Hussaini,
who died in A.D. 1615. Persian influence predominates in the rendering of
nature, and the painting has long been considered an example of Mughal art.
Recently it has been reattributed to Golconda in the Deccan. Whatever its
provenance, it is one of the finest paintings in the museum's Indian collection.

DURGĀ AS THE SLAYER OF THE BUFFALO DEMON. Dark granulite. India,
Pallava, eighth century. H. 1.5 m. *Denman Waldo Ross Collection. 27.171*
The goddess with eight arms stands triumphant in graceful *déhanchement*
(*tribhaṅga*) on the head of the buffalo demon she has destroyed. Among the
recognizable attributes are the trident, the sword, the discus, the conch, and
the bow on the left. In her emanation as Mahiṣāsuramardinī, Durgā is worshipped in India as the symbol of Primordial Energy, triumphant over evil, per-
sonified by the demon. The sculpture is a superb example of the Pallava style
that had matured by the late seventh century, as is apparent from the Mamal-
lapuram monuments. The Pallava artists developed a sophisticated artistic idiom
of their own that combined the earlier Andhra tradition of slim and elegantly
proportioned figures with a dynamic vitality that was probably inspired by
the Hindu themes.

HEAD OF A BUDDHA. Andesite. Chandi Sewu (Central Java), late eighth century A.D.   H. 38.7 cm. *Gift of the Honorable George Holden Tinkham. 43.6*
This head of a Buddha is a typical example of the classical Central Javanese type, derived from Indian Gupta prototypes. Most of the Buddha heads of this type in Western collections are said to have come from the great Buddhist sanctuary Barabudur. This head is one of the very few examples that can be attributed with confidence to the other great Buddhist temple complex of Central Java, Chandi Sewu. Its present name, literally meaning "Thousand Temples," is a slight exaggeration, for this giant complex actually consisted of about 250 temple buildings, arranged in four concentric squares around a large central sanctuary. In 1960 one of the subsidiary temples on the east side was found to contain a dedicatory inscription bearing a date corresponding to A.D. 792. At the time Congressman Tinkham acquired the head during the early thirties several statues in situ were still intact. The last Buddha head disappeared from the site in 1969. With its soft, rounded features, its introspective expression, the prominent protuberance on the head (Sanskrit: *uṣnīṣa*), and the hair consisting of regularly arranged curls, the head displays the typical iconographic and stylistic characteristics of Buddhist art of Java during its golden age.

TWO APOTHECARIES. From a manuscript of Dioscorides, *Materia Medica.*
Mesopotamia, dated in accordance with A.D. 1224.   25 x 33 cm. *Goloubew Collection, Francis Bartlett Donation, and Picture Fund. 14.536*
In this page from an Arabic translation of a Greek scientific treatise two apothecaries stand on either side of a jar discussing the preparation of medicine. While the *Materia Medica* of Dioscorides was orginally translated into Arabic in the ninth century A.D. by Hundin b. Ishaq, this version was written by the scribe 'Abdullah b. al-Fazl in 1224 A.D. and illustrated by an unknown artist. The composition of this painting probably was based on a Byzantine prototype with its minimal spatial definition and yet expressively depicted figures. This page is one of thirty-one leaves of the manuscript dispersed in Western collections.

EWER. Brass inlaid with silver. Iran, early 13th century.   H. 47.8 cm. *Holmes Collection. 49.1901*
Fluted in ten vertical lobes, the body of this ewer is inlaid with silver and covered with animal and human motifs. The high, curving spout has a hinged cover, and the neck is adorned with crouching lions in fairly high relief. The neck, handle, and base are inscribed with benedictions in Naskhi script. Around the main section of the body are five registers of decoration, including harpies, musicians, arabesques, and medallions with hunting scenes. These decorative motifs reflect the life at court where this sumptuous ewer was perhaps used.

SILVER CANDLESTICK. Iran, dated in accordance with A.D. 1129.   H. 44.5 cm., diam. 42.4 cm. *Holmes Collection. 48.1283*
The dated silver candlestick is an object of majestic size and proportions. According to its inscription, it was made by Abu'l Fath b. Hassan b. Sa'id Moradi and was presented to the sacred shrine of the Imam Reza at Masshad in 523 A.H./1129 A.D. during the reign of Sultan Sanjar (ruled A.D. 1118-1157). Not only from the royal form of the inscription but also from the refinement of design one can conclude that Abu'l Fath was a leading metal-worker of the period, who worked for Sultan Sanjar, a noted patron of the arts. The well-balanced design of this piece consists of bands of floriated Kufic script, scrollwork, and trefoil lobes. The Kufic writing is of special interest for its decorative quality; the tops of the vertical letters resemble strangely grinning faces with pointed noses. A scientific examination of this piece has revealed that the metal is an alloy consisting largely of silver and minute quantities of copper and gold. The piece was constructed in three parts: the base, the stem, and the sconce. The base was formed by hammering out a solid piece of silver into a hollow drum-shaped ring. The round top with its stem and sconce was brazed onto the base.

LUSTERWARE BOWL. Iran, early 13th century. H. 9.3 cm., diam. 20.9 cm.
Holmes Collection. 50.3629
This bowl with its two seated figures and two bands of Naskhi script is a fine
example of the thirteenth century luster-painted ware of Kashan. The figure on
the left is clad in a striped dress with a checkered hat, while the figure on the
right wears a robe decorated with scrolls and dots. The poses of the figures,
leaning slightly inward, and their moon-shaped faces set off by haloes echo the
round form of the bowl itself. The outside of the bowl is decorated with
vertical stripes, dots, and curved lines.

LUSTERWARE TILE. Signed Abu Rufaza. Iran, dated in accordance with September, A.D. 1211. Diam. 28.5 cm. *Ross Collection. 07.903*
An early example of Kashan lusterware tiles, this tile is typical of this kind of
ware both in subject matter and style. Here a hunter on horseback is shown
with his two dogs beside him. The birds and scrolling arabesques in the background are common features of Kashan lusterware tiles.

PORTRAIT OF SHAH TAHMASP. Iran, Safavid period, 16th century. 12.8 x 31.3
cm. *Goloubew Collection, Francis Bartlett Donation, and Picture Fund. 14.590*
This painting, most likely a portrait of Shah Tahmasp (ruled 1524-1576), was
painted by Sultan Muhammad, a leading painter at the Safavid court in Tabriz.
The refinement of the era is reflected in the precise, subtle detail of this
painting, as, for example, the rope falling from the Shah's waist, which curls
gracefully around his dagger.

BATTLE OF ALEXANDER AND THE DRAGON. Leaf from a *Shah Namah*. Iran,
14th century. 29.2 x 17.5 cm. *Denman Waldo Ross Collection. 30.105*
The Battle of Alexander and the Dragon from a dispersed manuscript, the
Demotte *Shah Namah*, is one of the finest examples of fourteenth century
Persian painting. Executed on a large scale, the paintings from this heroic
manuscript reveal the influence of both the Chinese and the Byzantine styles.
In this painting the background relies on Chinese prototypes, while Alexander
and his army are depicted in a more realistic, modeled fashion, related to the
Byzantine and Mesopotamian styles. Although the legend above the miniature
reads "Alexander in Combat with the Rhinoceros," the beast depicted here is
a composite form with the horn of a rhinoceros, wings of an eagle, claws of
a lion, and fangs of a wolf. Such a free interpretation of the text of the epic
results in the forceful and heroic composition of this and many of the other
miniatures from the Demotte *Shah Namah*.

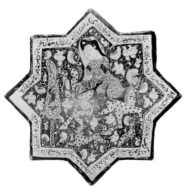

DEPARTMENT OF CLASSICAL ART

Classical art in the museum ranks high among all similar collections. Although surpassed in size by those of the great national museums of Europe, this collection is considered to be outstanding for its high artistic quality and its almost complete freedom from commonplace objects.

The entire range of Greek, Roman, and Etruscan art is encompassed. Even distant ages from which little has survived are represented by works of outstanding merit, such as the *Minoan Snake Goddess* of about 1600 B.C., the bronze *Deer Nursing Her Fawn* from the Geometric period, and the *Kypselid Gold Bowl* from the seventh century B.C. The collection is particularly strong in objects of the sixth, fifth, and fourth centuries B.C. The group of archaic bronze figurines is almost unequalled outside of Greece, for example, and the red-figured vases permit an extraordinarily comprehensive survey of the work produced by the major painters of fifth century Athens. Also from the fifth century is the three-sided relief, one of the greatest pieces of sculpture to survive from antiquity. In the fourth century and the Hellenistic period it is the sculpture that is of greatest importance, because the collection contains an unusually large number of original works by gifted Greek artists. Roman copies of Greek statues are relatively few, and the sculpture of the Roman period consists chiefly of excellent portraits. Objects of interest and importance may also be found among the terracotta figurines, jewelry, and ancient glass. Finally, two special collections may be mentioned: the Greek coins, a small but carefully selected series of examples of

VOTIVE DOUBLE-AXE. Gold, Minoan, ca. 1500 B.C.   W. 3¾ in. *Theodora Wilbour Fund in memory of Zoë Wilbour. 58.1009*
Found in a cave on Crete, this axe bears an inscription in Linear A script, a dedication to a Cretan goddess.

great rarity and artistic value, and the famous Warren collection of ancient cameo and intaglio gems.

The formation of the collection was the result almost completely of gift and purchase. In 1872 the museum acquired its first classical antiquities when a collection of objects from Cyprus was purchased from General di Cesnola. Gifts of varying merit soon followed, and a series of worthy but for the most part minor objects came to the museum from excavations in Assos, Naucratis, Argos, and Cyrene. But the collection as such was formed in the two decades 1890 to 1910, an extraordinary achievement made possible by the donations of a number of generous Boston people. The names that recur most often are Catharine Page Perkins, Henry Lillie Pierce, and Francis Bartlett. The actual finding and acquiring of the objects, however, was the work of one man, Edward Perry Warren. A wealthy and learned connoisseur, Warren devoted many years to the assembling of the collection, and as it stands, it is in large part a monument to his great knowledge and superb taste. The museum is fortunate that he became interested in developing the collection at a time when works of art of the first magnitude were available, and when donors could provide the great sums required. In succeeding years, the late Lacey D. Caskey, long curator of the department, added a number of pieces as they became available, each of them important for the rounding out of the collection and each showing his exquisite taste.

Additional works of Greek, Etruscan, and Roman art have been added in the generation since Mr. Caskey's death, and at present efforts are being made to insure that ancient art is comprehensively represented and intelligently displayed. The department has an extensive publication program designed to produce guides, catalogues, and picture books on specific sections, from vases to sculptured portraits to Greek and Roman coins. There is also a handbook of the classical collection, titled *Greek, Etruscan, and Roman Art*, in which art from the Bronze Age to Byzantium is surveyed against the rich background of the department. Other general publications currently available at the museum include *Greek Gods and Heroes* (1969), *Greek and Roman Portraits, 470 B.C.-A.D. 500* (M.F.A. Picture Book no. 14, 1972), *Greek, Etruscan & Roman Bronzes* (1971), and *Attic Black-figured Amphorae* (1973). The latest publications are *Catalogue of Greek Coins* (1974), *Roman Medallions* (1975), *Arretine Pottery* (1975), and *Ancient Gems* (Warren Collection) (1975).

CYCLADIC STATUETTE. Marble, ca. 2500-2000 B.C.   H. 6½ in. *William Amory Gardner Fund. 35.60*
This primitive representation of a woman made in the Cyclades Islands is an example of the earliest class of figural sculpture from Bronze Age Greece. These funerary "idols" were perhaps made to be viewed horizontally.

SNAKE GODDESS. Gold and ivory, ca. 1600-1500 B.C.   H. 6½ in. *Gift of Mrs. W. Scott Fitz. 14.863*
Very few examples of sculpture in the round have survived from the great Minoan civilization in Crete, and this exquisite figure is by far the finest piece known. Probably part of the palace treasury at Knossos, she represented the mother goddess of Aegean religion and protected the royal household of the king.

MYCENAEAN LIBATION VASE. Kernos, from Rhodes, 13th century B.C.   H. 4¼
in. *Otis Norcross Fund. 35.735*
A pair of doves perch on the twisted basket handle of the vase. Liquids poured
into the little jars on the circle (two of the original five are missing) would run
down into the body of the vase and out through the three holes in the mouth
of the bull's head. Such complex vessels were used in the ceremonies of Late
Bronze Age sanctuaries from the Peloponnesus to Cyprus and were also placed
in tombs.

GEOMETRIC PITCHER. Attic oinochoe, late ninth century B.C.   H. 8¾ in.
Catharine Page Perkins Fund. 97.360
The character of the decoration has given its name to both the ware and the
period in which the pottery was made. The formal decorative patterns include
parallel lines, concentric circles, zigzags, and crosshatching.

DEER NURSING HER FAWN. Bronze, from Thebes, eighth century B.C.   H. 2⅞
in. *H. L. Pierce Fund. 98.650*
A bird sits on the back of the deer. The angularity of the figures and the engraved concentric circles indicate that the bronze is contemporary with geometric pottery and is thus a very early example of the sculpture produced by the
people of Iron Age Greece.

MAGICAL WHEEL. Terracotta, Attic, late eighth century B.C.   D. 11½ in.
John Michael Rodocanachi Fund. 28.49
Such wheels were supposed to have magical properties when rotated. They were
spun on cords, suggesting that this example in terracotta was not made for actual
use. It was probably an offering in a temple. The bird represented is the iynx or
European wry-neck, and the piece is known as the iynx wheel.

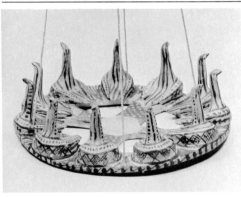

STATUETTE OF APOLLO. Bronze, ca. 700 B.C. H. 8 in. *Francis Bartlett Collection.* *03.997*
The inscription in very early Boeotian letters records this as a dedication by one Mantiklos to Apollo. Still awkwardly proportioned, the figure nonetheless shows a solidity and roundness far in advance of the work of the geometric period.

LATE CORINTHIAN COLUMN KRATER. Mixing vessel, ca. 540-525 B.C. H. 13 in. *Helen and Alice Colburn Fund and gift in memory of Stephen B. Luce. 63.420*
Herakles (or is the god Apollo?) fires his arrows at a colorful dragon in his cave under the sea, while his lady companion Hesione hurls rocks. Beyond the mythological scene, at the left, a charioteer gallops his quadriga of one white and three black horses away from the assault. The dragon had threatened Hesione, in one of the typical sagas of a maiden rescued from a monster by a hero. A procession of bearded elders is shown on the other side of the vase.

ATTIC BLACK-FIGURED WINE JAR. Amphora, ca. 540 B.C., by the BMN Painter. H. 15½ in. *Otis Norcross Fund. 60.1*
Theseus is shown killing the Minotaur, watched by Ariadne and two youths. The unfortunate creature sinks to his right knee, a stone held in the raised left hand. The woman, who must be Ariadne, daughter of King Minos, watches in horror, while the two richly clad young men stand with spears in hand, typifying the elegant aristocrats of Athens at the height of the Archaic period. The artist has been identified as the British Museum Nikosthenes Painter, from a vase signed by the potter Nikosthenes in that collection. The other side of the vase shows the heavenly twins (Dioskouroi), Kastor and Polydeukes, arriving home on horseback in the presence of Poseidon and members of their family.

THE "ORIENTAL ARTEMIS," MISTRESS OF ANIMALS. Electrum repoussé plaque, from Kameiros on Rhodes, ca. 600 B.C. H. 2⅜ in. *H. L. Pierce Fund. 99.383*
The early Archaic motif was popular throughout the East Greek world. This small plaque is one of a group that formed a necklace or a girdle or that perhaps was simply sewed onto a woman's clothing as decoration.

CLASSICAL ART | 79

ATTIC BLACK-FIGURED PYXIS. Container for precious objects, mid-sixth century B.C. H. 3⅞ in. *Gift of Horace L. Mayer. 61.1256a,b*
In a wide frieze between bands of dots, Apollo and Herakles struggle for possession of the Delphic tripod while an assembly of gods and goddesses watches. On the lid, amid filling ornaments and encircled by ivy leaves, there are a lion, a goat, and a pair of Sirens. Heads are large and feet are loosely painted, but black glaze topped with reds and white produces courtliness in the idiom of Archaic directness that makes this pyxis a charming survivor of Attic minor art.

GOLD BOWL. From Olympia, late seventh century B.C. D. 6¼ in. *Francis Bartlett Fund. 21.1843*
At the rim is an inscription in the early Corinthian alphabet stating that this bowl was dedicated by the sons of Kypselos from the spoils of Herakleia. Kypselos was the rich and famous tyrant of Corinth in the seventh century B.C., but the battle of Herakleia is otherwise unknown. The shape is that of a libation bowl, with a central boss to make it easier to hold for pouring.

ATTIC BLACK-FIGURED BAND CUP. Ca. 540 B.C. D. 9 in. *William E. Nickerson Fund, No. 2. 61.1073*
Various animals in combat and Sirens appear on both sides of the cup. The animals have their names individually inscribed. Illustrated here are a Siren, a lion attacking a boar, two leopards biting on a deer, and another Siren. The cup is signed on each side by the potter Neandros. The animal groups of these elegant little friezes are inspired in a general way from the pedimental sculptures of the Archaic temples on and near the Acropolis of Athens.

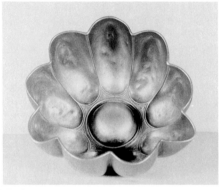

STATUETTE OF ARTEMIS. Bronze, from Mazi, near Olympia, about 525 B.C. H. 7½ in. *H. L. Pierce Fund. 98.658*
Dedicated by Chimaridas to the "Daidalian" goddess. Half her bow is missing. The left hand also probably held an arrow. The neat Laconian (Spartan) lettering appears vertically on the front of her long garment. The conservative costume, traditional stance, and other details of this charming figure are also Laconian.

WOMEN AT A FOUNTAIN HOUSE. Detail of an Attic black-figured hydria (water jar). H. 21¼ in. *William Francis Warden Fund. 61.195*
This late sixth century vase shows a scene related to its function. Women are dancing and talking as they fill similar hydriae from spouts, within the columned facade of the fountain. The spouts take various forms, the head of a lion on the left, that of a donkey on the right. Such fountain houses are still to be seen at Megara near Athens and at Lindos on the island of Rhodes.

ATTIC BLACK-FIGURED WINE JAR. Amphora, about 540 B.C., by the potter Exekias. H. 20½ in. *Henry Lillie Pierce Residuary Fund and Bartlett Collection by Exchange. 63.952*
The wine god Dionysos is shown seated under a carpet-like grapevine filled with playing satyrs. He is tasting the wine from a high-handled, long-stemmed cup (kantharos), which the twelve diminutive satyrs have been preparing from the grapes in the three baskets in front of and behind the god. Exekias, both as painter and potter, was one of the great masters of Attic black-figured vases at the height of their production. The painter of this amphora was either a very close associate of Exekias or perhaps the master himself.

AN ETRUSCAN LEOPARD. Nenfro, ca. 560 B.C.   H. 24¼ in. *William Francis Warden Fund. 61.130*
Carved in volcanic stone (nenfro), this svelte beast typifies the best of archaic Etruscan funerary sculpture. It probably adorned the lintel of a tomb at Vulci. The leopard is exhibited high on the wall in the Etruscan gallery together with its mate, facing in the opposite direction (gift of Horace L. Mayer. 63.2756). A considerably larger, more ferocious leopard of this general type of monumental Etruscan sculpture in nenfro is also in the gallery, as are a similar lion, two female sphinxes, and a hippocamp (sea horse).

SPHINX. Marble, ca. 535-530 B.C.   H. 55¾ in. *1931 and 1939 Purchase Funds. 40.576*
The sphinx and volutes once formed the crowning member of a tall grave monument. The workmanship is Attic. Traces of blue, red, green, and black paint remain on the wings, breast, and volutes. This is the finest example of the several similar sphinx monuments that exist. The lower part of the flat, rectangular shaft with the feet of an armed warrior in low relief and the praedella panel with the warrior's chariot appears to be in the Metropolitan Museum of Art, New York. Boston also possesses pieces of the stepped base with the dedicatory inscription.

ATTIC RED-FIGURED PLATE. Ca. 520 B.C., by the Cerberus Painter. D. 7½ in.
H. L. Pierce Fund. 01.8025
Herakles, wearing the skin of the Nemean lion, is shown dragging Cerberus up
from the underworld, with Hermes in attendance, his caduceus in his right hand.

STATUETTE OF HERMES KRIOPHOROS. Bronze, 520-510 B.C. H. 6½ in.
H. L. Pierce Fund. 04.6
This figure of Hermes "the ram-carrier" is the smaller of two similar statuettes in
the collection. The small ram in the god's left hand suggests the statuette is a
votive offering to Hermes as protector of flocks.

HERAKLES WRESTLING WITH TRITON. Attic black-figured water jar, ca. 530-520
B.C., by the Chiusi Painter. H. 19¼ in. *Gift of Horace L. Mayer. 62.1185*
Nereus and one of his Nereid daughters watch this epic struggle between the
hero in his lion's skin and the fish-tailed old Triton. Herakles is about to squeeze
from Triton the whereabouts of the Golden Apples of the Hesperides. On the
shoulder of the hydria (not illustrated) two four-horse chariots move in stately
procession to the right, each watched by a seated youth.

A GOD, HERO OR VOTARY. Life-sized head, from a statue in light stone, 520-
500 B.C. Found by Luigi Palma di Cesnola at Golgoi (Athienou) or Idalion (Dali)
on Cyprus. H. 10½ in. *Purchase by subscription. 72.322*
The forceful youth, of divine or heroic nature, wears an ornamented band above
his forehead and an elaborate cloth cap, not unlike the lion's skin of Herakles
(see the previous) behind this. This head has been carved in the best East Greek,
Cypriote (Ionian) Late Archaic style and ought to represent a mythological (?)
figure of note.

ATTIC RED-FIGURED CUP. Kylix, ca. 520-510 B.C.   D. 9⅜ in. *H. L. Pierce Fund.*
00.336
The decoration in the bottom of the cup shows an archer inspecting his arrow.
The youth wears a chiton, quiver, and cross-belt.

STATUETTE OF ATHENA. Bronze, from Minorca, ca. 500 B.C.   H. 4¼ in.
William E. Nickerson Fund No. 2. 54.145
The goddess is shown in her role of warrior and protector of the city. While
probably produced in a workshop in Athens, this late Archaic Athena Promachos
is one of the finest early Greek bronzes to have been found in or close to Spain.

ACHILLES DRAGGING THE BODY OF HECTOR AROUND THE WALLS OF TROY.
Attic black-figured water jar, ca. 510 B.C.   H. 20½ in. *William Francis Warden
Fund. 63.473*
In this crowded scene of action and tragedy, Hector's parents, Priam and
Hecuba, mourn in their palace within the citadel of Troy as vengeful Achilles
stares at them. (Queen Hecuba's head alone is visible beside the dark-garbed
king.) Hector, dragged behind the chariot, is identified by an inscription just
above his body. The winged messenger goddess Iris, the soul of Patroclus (in the
form of a small, winged warrior), and a sacred snake move in front of the large,
white, inscribed tomb-mound of Patroclus at the right. On the shoulder, two
four-horsed chariots gallop from left to right, one driven by Athena. Between
them, Herakles pursues the robber Kyknos, while Ares rushes from the left. The
full decorative richness of black-figure painting is seen in its latest phase, at the
end of the Archaic period.

KNEELING ARCHER. Gem, chalcedony intaglio, ca. 500 B.C., attributed to
Epimenes.   L. ¾ in. Enlarged. *Francis Bartlett Fund. 21.1194*
The youth's complex pose is related to the circular (tondo) interiors of early
red-figured cups.

HANDLE OF A MIRROR. Bronze, ca. 480 B.C.   H. 10½ in. *Purchased by
Contribution. 01.7499*
The modeling shows a great advance over sixth century sculpture, but the
precise coiffure and decorative folds of the garment are still in an Archaic
style. The low footstool has hooves for feet. The attachment for the missing
mirror consists of two tendrils ending in volutes.

KANTHAROS.   H. 9¾ in. *Catharine Page Perkins Fund. 95.36*
The cup, of the early fifth century B.C., is obviously modeled after a metal
kantharos of exceptionally beautiful, though simple form. The tall handles are
thin and flat, like bands of metal. On one side is represented Zeus pursuing a
nymph, on the other Zeus pursuing Ganymede, who has been playing with hoop
and stick. The vigorous style of drawing is found on a number of vases signed
by the potter Brygos, and this kantharos, though unsigned, is surely the work of
the most skillful artist in his employ, the so-called Brygos Painter.

DEMARETEION. Silver coin of Syracuse, slightly enlarged. D. 35 mm. *Theodora Wilbour Fund in memory of Zoë Wilbour. 35.21*
On the obverse are a victorious four-horse chariot and a lion symbolizing the victory of the Syracusans over the Carthaginians in 480 B.C.; on the reverse, the head of Arethusa, patron goddess of Syracuse. The coin is named for the queen of Syracuse, Demarete. This piece is considered by many to be the most beautiful specimen of the most beautiful coin ever designed by the Greeks.

COIN OF LEONTINI. Silver tetradrachm, ca. 479 B.C. D. 26.5 mm. *Theodora Wilbour Fund in memory of Zoë Wilbour. 55.963*
On the obverse, a chariot moves to the right, the charioteer being crowned by a Nike. Below the groundline a lion runs right. The reverse is a head of Apollo, also with a lion below. The tetradrachm was probably struck for the same occasion as the Demareteion.

BOAR. Bronze, ca. 480 B.C. L. 6⅜ in. *James Fund and special contribution. 10.162*
This figure together with a companion lion once rested on the rim of a very large bronze vessel, evidently found in the marshes of Ancona or near Sirolo. The curved supporting band has been broken away between the animal's front and hind feet. Fine, incised lines have been used to indicate the bristles of this spirited, late Archaic boar at bay. The artist who fashioned this animal was probably a Greek from the northern Peloponnesus or Tarentum.

THREE-SIDED RELIEF. Rectangular marble sculpture, ca. 470-460 B.C., found in Rome. H. 38 in. *H. L. Pierce Fund. 08.205*

On the front, a winged figure holding a balance stands between a pensive woman on the right and a cheerful one on the left. On the end piece at the left is an old woman, and on the other a young man playing the lyre. The scene may represent Eros judging a contest for Adonis between Persephone and Aphrodite. This sculpture is the counterpart of a similarly shaped marble in Rome, the so-called Ludovisi Throne, and the two may once have been the sculptured decoration of the two wings framing the steps of a very large altar of Aphrodite. The two three-sided reliefs were evidently made for a Greek city of southern Italy and brought to Rome as collectors' items in antiquity. They were both excavated, at different dates late in the nineteenth century, during building operations on the Ludovisi family estate on the Pincian Hill in Rome. In antiquity this area had been the Gardens of Sallust. The differences in style between these reliefs and those in the Museo Nazionale, Rome, has been explained by the suggestion that a master sculptor made the "Ludovisi Throne," while a more up-to-date or later pupil carved the "Boston Counterpart."

MOUNTED WARRIOR. Marble grave relief, Attic, ca. 500-490 B.C.   H. 32 in.
H. L. Pierce Fund. 99.339
Certain grooves and holes show where bronze reins were once attached. Elegantly carved in the sculptural traditions of Attica at the end of the Archaic
period, the very high relief shows the knight in his crested Attic helmet, cloak,
and short tunic. The horse was turning his head outwards toward the spectator.
The stele was found near Thebes in Boeotia, just over the northeastern border
from Attica.

THE FALL OF TROY. Attic red-figured krater, ca. 465 B.C., by the Altamura
Painter.   H. 18⅞ in. *William Francis Warden Fund. 59.178*
Cassandra is being dragged from the Palladion by Ajax the Less. At the right,
Neoptolemos, son of Achilles, hurls Astyanax from the city's walls, while aged
Priam pleads vainly from the palace altar. Beyond, at the right, can be seen
two warriors facing each other (perhaps Agamemnon restraining his brother
Menelaos from killing Helen). The other side of this large-scale composition
features a young warrior (perhaps Askanios, Aeneas' son) or the god Hermes
leading Aeneas and his aged father Anchyses from burning Troy. Ill-fated
Creusa follows behind. All these various scenes were probably taken from
famous mural paintings in Athens of the time of the Persian Wars.

STATUETTE OF A RUNNING GIRL ("Lasa"). Bronze, perhaps Campanian of the early fifth century B.C. H. 5⅛ in. *H. L. Pierce Fund. 98.662*
If not made in one of the southernmost cities of Etruria, or in Latium, this Etruscan concept of a running spirit or soul was produced in a Campanian Greek workshop for the Etruscan market.

FIGURINE OF A MAN COOKING. Terracotta, Boeotian, late sixth century B.C. H. 4⅛ in. *Catharine Page Perkins Fund. 97.349*
This figure and its companion pieces (such as a girl cooking, a barber cutting a customer's hair, and a woman kneading bread) permit an unusually candid view of the everyday life of the Greek people. These figures may well be called the ancestors of the famous Tanagra figurines of later days. They were found in tombs and as dedicatory offerings in temples.

DEATH OF AGAMEMNON. Attic red-figured krater, ca. 460 B.C., by the Dokimasia Painter. H. 19 in. *William Francis Warden Fund. 63.1246*
On this krater the *Oresteia* erupts with hurricane force. Aigisthos, tall, bearded, in the prime of life, has already struck Agamemnon, and as he sinks backward Aigisthos steadies him for the death blow. Klytaimnestra lifts a double axe to hit her husband if her lover should miss. Women enframe this broadly conceived scene with gestures of terror and amazement. On the side of the vase not illustrated Orestes kills Aigisthos, encouraged by Elektra. Klytaimnestra, again shown with her axe, is unable to prevent this act of revenge. This krater, the work of a painter otherwise noted for his decoration of much smaller cups, forms a worthy thematic companion to the Fall of Troy vase by the nearly contemporary Altamura Painter.

PORTRAIT SIGNED BY DEXAMENOS. Gem, red and yellow jasper intaglio, third quarter of the fifth century B.C. L. 21 mm. *Francis Bartlett Fund. 23.580*
Dexamenos was one of the most famous gem-cutters of this period. The portrait gem is remarkable for its individual character at a time when most artists were producing very idealized features.

WOMAN WITH A MIRROR. Marble grave monument, probably made in Athens near the end of the fifth century B.C. H. 23¼ in. *H. L. Pierce Fund. 04.16*
The lady wears a sleeved chiton with overfold reaching to the waist and a himation. Her hair is bound up, and the back of her head is covered by a veil.

ATTIC RED-FIGURED WINE JAR. Stamnos, third quarter of the fifth century B.C. H. 16 in. *Catharine Page Perkins Fund. 95.21*
Such intimate domestic scenes became popular subjects for vase painting in the later fifth century. Hand mirrors are hanging on the walls, and the women congregate around a large basin on a stand. The servant girl at the extreme right holds up an elaborate perfume jar. This stamnos, then, becomes an excellent pictorial illustration of how the Athenians used the utensils and vessels exhibited today in the museums of the world.

GOLD BROOCH. Fibula or pin for a dress with filigree decoration, probably Campanian of the fourth century B.C. L. 3½ in. One of a pair. *H. L. Pierce Fund. 99.371*

The central design consists of a rosette superimposed on a foliate pattern in the shape of a star, leading to an architectural palmette at each end. Other rosettes are mounted on the pointed ends of the almond-shaped arc of the main element. Greek artists in the cities around the Bay of Naples and to the south created such jewelry for local markets and for the Etruscans.

ATTIC RED-FIGURED WINE JAR. Pelike, ca. 440 B.C., by the Lycaon Painter. H. 18¾ in. *William Amory Gardner Fund. 34.79*

The scene is taken from the *Odyssey,* when Odysseus sacrifices two rams in the underworld; at the left, the shade of his former companion, Elpenor, rises up from the ground, originally indicated by white lines. At the right appears Hermes, the messenger god who traditionally conducts people and souls to (or from) the underworld. The Lycaon Painter has been influenced by major masters of mural painting, such as Polygnotos, in his use of foreshortening and implications of perspective in an irregular landscape.

DOUBLE-SIDED VOTIVE RELIEF. Helios in his chariot. Attic, ca. 340 B.C. H. 17¾ in., w. 17½ in. (as preserved). *Frederick Brown Fund. 1972.78*

Helios in a long chiton, a nimbus (halo) behind his head, drives the four horses of the sun across the front of the relief's architectural niche. The composition was developed in Greek painting in the last quarter of the fifth century B.C. The sculptor of this scene worked at the time when leading Greek masters, such as Skopas, were carving similar chariot groups for the small frieze of the mausoleum at Halicarnassus in southwest Asia Minor, one of the Seven Wonders of the ancient world. On the second side of the relief, the Asian moon-god Mên is seated side saddle on a ram. In front, a table with votive offerings is approached by two bearded men, a youth, and a child.

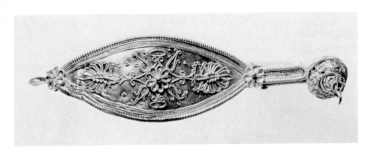

GOLD EARRING. Mid-fourth century B.C. H. 2 in. *H. L. Pierce Fund. 98.788*
The large size and the subject of a Victory driving a two-horse chariot make it likely that the earring was once a dedication to a goddess. Although evidently found in a tomb, the exquisitely fashioned little sculpture was perhaps designed to be displayed from the ear of a large cult statue. Some scholars have suggested the subject is not Nike driving her biga, but Psyche (the soul) racing heavenward.

COIN OF SYRACUSE. Silver dekadrachm, 413-387 B.C., signed by Euainetos. D. 36 mm. *H. L. Pierce Fund. 04.536*
The obverse presents a victorious four-horse chariot and prize armor in the area below. The reverse shows a head of the nymph Arethusa, surrounded by dolphins.

ATTIC WHITE-GROUND OIL BOTTLE. Lekythos, ca. 440 B.C., by the Achilles Painter. H. 12⅞ in. *Gift of E. P. Warren. 93.106*
Vases such as this, with figures painted in warm colors on a white surface, were the customary grave offerings in the late fifth century, and the scenes, as here, depict mourners bringing offerings to the grave. The slender stele is ornamented with a looped fillet in dull black paint on the lower step and another draped around the base; traces of two other fillets appear on the stele itself. On the right of the stele (not illustrated here) stands a woman holding a fillet or a wreath. The woman at the left brings a perfume vase to the tomb.

HEAD OF A GODDESS. Marble, from Chios, late fourth century B.C.   H. 14⅛ in. *Gift of Nathaniel Thayer. 10.70*
The head was once covered by the folds of a mantle worked in separate pieces of marble. A superb sculpture from about the time of Praxiteles, showing the soft impressionistic treatment typical of his later work.

HEAD OF ZEUS. Marble, from Mylasa, Caria, fourth century B.C.   H. 18⅛ in. *H. L. Pierce Fund. 04.12*
This over life-sized sculpture was carved by one of the major Greek masters of about 350 B.C., evidently as part of a cult-image of the Carian Zeus. Two holes in the head suggest the god wore a metal *polos* or "stovepipe" crown and an unusual costume traditional to the area. This concept of Zeus was based directly on the Zeus by Pheidias at Olympia nearly a hundred years earlier.

VOTIVE RELIEF TO HERAKLES ALEXIKAKOS. Marble, ca. 375-350 B.C.   H. 20⅞ in., w. 27⅜ in. *Catharine Page Perkins Fund. 96.696*
Herakles "Averter of Evil" and Hermes as a fellow god of the Greek gymnasium stand beside the former's shrine, in Athens. Herakles has draped the skin of the Nemean lion over his left arm while Hermes wears a cloak around his shoulders. The inscription on the shrine is a dedication to Herakles as the "Averter of Evil." Found in the Piraeus, this relief reflects the athletic canons of Athenian sculpture under the influence of both Pheidias and Polykleitos in the first half of the fourth century B.C.

HEAD OF APHRODITE. Marble, late fourth century B.C.   H. 14½ in. *Francis Bartlett Collection. 03.743*
Known as the Bartlett head of Aphrodite, after the donor, this presentation of the goddess is very close to the work of Praxiteles, and has generally been considered one of the most beautiful pieces of Greek sculpture in existence.

PAINTED TERRACOTTA PLAQUES. Etruscan, ca. 470 B.C.   H. 44 in. *William Francis Warden Fund. 62.362 and 62.363*

A female player of the lyre walks on a broad band with a maeander below. She holds her instrument by a cloth strap attached to her left wrist and a wavy plant rises at her feet. Her costume is elegant in the Late Archaic manner. The colors are red, blue-black, and (surface) green on white ground.

This presentation of a wreathed, male player of the double flutes was made as a pendant to the lady lyricist. He is more sober and restrained, and even the plant beyond is thin and severe. The two plaques were painted and fired much like Greek or Etruscan vases. They were pinned, in the order shown here, with iron pegs on the natural stone walls of a tomb, presumably in the necropolis of Vulci northwest of Rome. When the iron pegs rusted away the plaques fell to the tomb's floor, smashing into many pieces, now recomposed.

BOY WITH HORSE. Etruscan bronze mirror, fourth century B.C.   D. 6 in. *H. L. Pierce Fund. 99.495*

The depth and foreshortening in the calligraphy of this decorative subject echo monumental painting in the Greek world around 350 B.C.

PAESTAN RED-FIGURED WINE JAR. Amphora by the Boston Orestes Painter, 330-310 B.C.   H. 20¼ in. *H. L. Pierce Fund. 99.540*

The scene shows Electra, Orestes, and Pylades meeting at the tomb of Agamemnon. Electra at the right holds offerings for the dead, a vase in her left hand and a fillet in her right. Pylades and Orestes wear high boots and each holds a spear and a traveler's cap. The tomb is represented by a white Ionic column, set on a brownish base. Above the central figures, on either side, is a Fury, to suggest the later madness of Orestes. A Siren above, on the neck of the vase, holds a mirror in her right hand and a flat basket in her left. In front of her is a small altar. Attic vase painting was imitated more or less skillfully in many parts of South Italy, and some of the most interesting, most imaginative painters worked at Paestum.

AMPHORA WITH LID. Etruscan, ca. 520 B.C.   H. 12½ in. *Frederick Brown Fund. 62.970*

Large eyes and entwined snakes dominate this combination of mystery and decoration. The eyes may be guardians of the wine inside, and the decorative concept based on the Greek motifs is something only an Etruscan could have conceived. The eyes have been taken from the designs on contemporary Attic skyphoi and cups. This rare amphora, in a nearly perfect state of preservation, has a decorative lid, of Attic type, preserved. A similar vase is in the museum at Leiden in the Netherlands.

CALYX KRATER. Etruscan (Faliscan), ca. 360 B.C.   H. 19¾ in. *J. H. and E. A. Payne Fund. 1970.487*
This large, richly decorated vase was made and painted by the Nazzano Painter in central Italy for the Etruscan market. The krater illustrates in panoramic fashion the divinities witnessing the discovery of Telephos in Agamemnon's palace at Mycenae. Telephos, King of Pergamon in western Asia Minor, came to Greece seeking cure for a wound accidentally inflicted by Achilles at the outset of the Trojan War. The elaborate scene, based on a lost play by Euripides, includes most of the major gods and goddesses and the family of Agamemnon, at the moment when Telephos threatened to kill Agamemnon's son Orestes unless he was given treatment for the mistaken injury. The action centers on the palace altar, where Telephos is seated with a knife in one hand and the royal infant in the other.

PORTRAIT OF ARSINOË II. Bronze, early third century B.C.   H. 10¼ in.
Catharine Page Perkins Fund. 96.712
Identification of this head is not absolutely certain, but it is probably the portrait of Arsinoë II, who married Lysimachus, king of Thrace, in 299-298 B.C., and later became wife of Ptolemy II in Egypt. The eyes, now lost, were made of other materials.

FIGURINE OF A DRAPED WOMAN. Terracotta, perhaps made in Tanagra (in Boeotia, northeast of Athens) in the third century B.C.   H. 7 in. *Purchased by contribution. 01.7824*
Traces of blue remain on the cloak, red on the fan, and red-brown on the hair. Such statuettes, ideal in nature, were placed in tombs.

LID OF AN ETRUSCAN SARCOPHAGUS. Peperino, from Vulci, ca. 300-280 B.C.
L. 83 in. *Athenaeum Loan 1281*
The lid is fashioned into a likeness of the deceased and his wife to insure the couple's companionship in the afterworld. They appear to be under a cover on a couch. The sculptor has given a flattened, restless quality to the drapery and has shown their feet as if in profile rather than viewed from the top. The body of the sarcophagus (not illustrated) is an elaborate scene of a betrothal or wedding with attendants carrying musical instruments, personal effects of the bride, including her jewel box, and a chair. The two short ends are chariot scenes, one of which, showing two women accompanied by a winged spirit of death, has been interpreted as a last journey. The fourth side was left undecorated, so presumably the sarcophagus was placed against a wall.

CLASSICAL ART | 113

HEAD OF HOMER. Marble, late Hellenistic or Graeco-Roman.   H. 16⅛ in.
H. L. Pierce Fund. 04.13
This powerful study of an aged, blind, but noble man almost certainly embodies
the artist's concept of the great poet. It is a likeness of what Homer ought to
have been, pseudo-naturalistic in the details of age and physical condition but at
the same time based on a divine, heroic approach to mankind. Homer lived long
before Greek art came to consider the problems of portraiture as we know the
art after centuries of Hellenistic, Roman, and Renaissance experience. This head
probably belonged to a seated statue of the bard, clad perhaps in tunic and
cloak.

SOCRATES. This head, found in Athens, was made about A.D. 150 after an original by the Greek sculptor Lysippos, ca. 330 B.C., or seventy years after the great Athenian philosopher's death.   H. 8 in. *Frederick Brown Fund. 60.45*
The head is small and may have been a herm-portrait. The nose was broken in antiquity and repaired with an iron pin, which still remains. The original statue showed the sage seated on a ceremonial chair, a himation or cloak thrown around his wrinkled old body. It may have been fashioned in bronze. The sculptor relied on older, ideal likenesses and literary traditions in his portrayal of Socrates, although Lysippos could have talked with people who knew the philosopher.

STATUETTE OF AN ACTOR. Bronze, Graeco-Roman period.   H. 4¼ in.
H. L. Pierce Fund. 98.677
The actor, who is shown in a declamatory pose, wears a mask and a typical
theatrical costume with tights and long-sleeved tunic.

STATUETTE OF ZEUS. Bronze, Graeco-Roman period.   H. 3¾ in. *H. L. Pierce
Fund. 98.678*
The right hand holds a thunderbolt; the left once held a scepter. This statuette
is a reflection of the image of Jupiter (Zeus) Capitolinus that was created for
the temple of that name on the Capitoline Hill in Rome.

PORTRAIT BUST. Marble, Hellenistic or Graeco-Roman period, perhaps ca. 50
B.C.   H. 20¼ in. *Catharine Page Perkins Fund. 97.288*
Undoubtedly a portrait of the comic poet Menander, although once believed by
some scholars to represent Virgil. A small bronze bust of this type bears the
inscription "Menandros" in Greek on its plinth, a seeming confirmation of the
traditional identification. This marble herm-shaped bust is one of the finest likenesses that has survived from antiquity.

APULIAN RED-FIGURED BELL-KRATER. South Italian Greek, about 375 B.C.
H. 11¼ in. *Otis Norcross Fund. 69.951*
Phlyax vases illustrate scenes from rustic comedies featuring actors wearing
padded costumes (*phlyakes*). This latest phase of Attic Old Comedy is represented by a scene from *The Thief Apprehended*. A young policeman with his
staff of office has caught an old thief red-handed with baskets containing baby
goats and a goose, tied to the carrying-yoke. The herm topped by cloak and
aryballos behind the young man suggests the thief was stopped in the garden
of a palaestra or gymnasium.

STATUE OF HERMES. Marble, from Capua, Graeco-Roman period.   H. 28⅛ in.
Catharine Page Perkins Fund. 95.67
The traces of wings in the hair and the quiet, rather melancholy aspect identify
the figure as Hermes in his role as guide of the souls to the underworld. The
statue dates to the end of the Roman Republic or to the Augustan age.

STATUETTE OF HERCULES. Marble, Roman copy of a statue of the fifth century
B.C.   H. 22½ in. *Francis Bartlett Fund. 14.733*
The original was a work very famous in antiquity, probably by the sculptor
Myron. It was probably a lifesized, or larger, statue in bronze and may have been
dedicated at the temple of Hera on Samos. This copy reflects a Hellenistic
intermediary, probably at Pergamon, for here Herakles appears to have been
contemplating his infant son Telephos being nursed by a deer in Arcadia.

POLYPHEMOS. Marble, Hellenistic, ca. 150 B.C. or later.   H. 16 in. *Gift in
honor of Edward W. Forbes from his friends. 63.120*
Powerful in concept, reflecting sculptures of the school of Pergamon, the one-
eyed Cyclops looks savagely at us as he once did at Odysseus and the mariners
imprisoned in his cave. The head is the remains of a colossal statue, perhaps a
harbor group and probably representing the blinding of Polyphemos preparatory
to the escape of Odysseus and his companions from the cave.

FRAGMENTARY STATUE OF APHRODITE. Marble, Graeco-Roman period.
H. 49¼ in. *H. L. Pierce Fund. 99.350*
This figure is one of the many ancient adaptations of a very popular statue
going back ultimately to an Aphrodite by Praxiteles. The type is known as the
Capitoline Venus from the famous Graeco-Roman copy in the municipal collections of Rome. Lysippos may have created the original in bronze about
325 B.C.

PORTRAIT OF A ROMAN. Palombino, first century B.C.   H. 13 in. *H. L. Pierce Fund. 99.343*

A very realistic study from the late Republican period in Rome. Palombino is a hard volcanic stone that was used in Rome chiefly at the end of the Republican period. The man has not been identified.

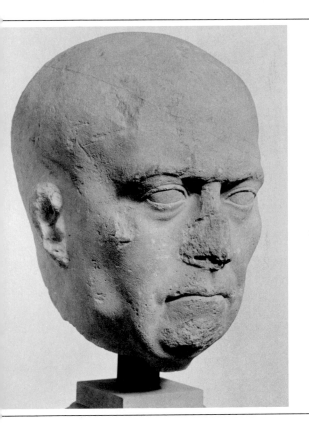

TERRACOTTA PORTRAIT OF A ROMAN. Late first century B.C.   H. 14 in.
Purchased by contribution. 01.8008
Realistic marble portraits are characteristic of the period, but this magnificent
example is made of clay and is so extraordinarily true to life that it is thought
that it may have been made with the use of a mask. The bust, doubtless a fami
heirloom, was found in the ruins of a villa at Cumae northwest of Naples. The
man may have been a Latin, but more likely he was an Oscan or local native
inhabitant who spoke Greek as well as his own tongue. Cumae had been a
prosperous Greek city.

PORTRAIT OF AUGUSTUS. Marble, first or second century A.D.   H. 17 in.
H. L. Pierce Fund. 99.344
This portrait of the emperor who ruled from 27 B.C. to A.D. 14 is strongly
idealized, yet it conveys much of the essential character of the man. It was made
as part of a draped statue. From the quasi-divine, Greek heroic quality imparted
to the hair, this likeness has been dated in the reign of Hadrian (A.D. 117 to 138).

LIVIA AND TIBERIUS. Gem, turquoise cameo, first century B.C. to first century A.D.   H. 1¼ in. *H. L. Pierce Fund. 99.109*
Livia, wife of Augustus, and her young son Tiberius, the second emperor (A.D. 14-37). The empress is represented in the guise of a goddess, perhaps Venus Genetrix, and she is apparently holding the bust of her son, heir to the throne new emperor, on her outstretched right hand.

PORTRAIT OF A SMALL BOY. Marble, second half of the first century A.D. H. 9½ in. *H. L. Pierce Fund. 01.8202*
The hair combed over the forehead combined with the abbreviated form of the draped bust identifies this sculpture as a creation of the time of Nero (A.D. 54-68).

A MAN OF CA. A.D. 280. He is perhaps the Roman Emperor Numerianus (A.D. 282-284).   H. 15½ in. *Otis Norcross Fund. 58.1005*
The large eyes and drilled-out hair are hallmarks of the decades when classical art was moving into its late Antique phase. The ill-fated young Emperor Numerianus was known as a phil-Hellene, a rare champion of Greek culture and literature in an era of barbarian invasions, civil wars, and military emperors. This portrait may have been commissioned by a Greek living near Rome.

DONKEY NURSING LION CUBS. Mosaic, found in Tunisia, executed about A.D. 400.   W. 60⅝ in. *Gift of the Class of the Museum. 60.531*
This unusual subject is a Bacchic parody of the Roman Wolf-and-Twins. It is also a symbolic reference to worship of Bacchus at a time when Christians were closing the pagan temples.

ROMAN FRESCO. From a villa in Boscotrecase, near Pompeii, first century A.D. H. 74¾ in. *Ellen Frances Mason Fund. 33.499*
One of a series of frescoes from the same house with fanciful architectural representations painted mainly in red and yellow. They were painted on the interior walls, beneath the colonnades, of a rectangular peristyle or garden court. Thus, they were best seen at a short distance, between the intervals of the columns.

FRAGMENT OF ROMANO-CAMPANIAN WALL PAINTING, Ca. A.D. 60
W. (max.) 18⅞ in. *Otis Norcross Fund. 1970.62*
The remains of decorative fresco from the wall of a Graeco-Roman villa, probably in Central Italy, this spirited rococo scene is painted in creamy whites, marine blue-greens, and yellowish browns on a "Pompeiian" red background. A chubby little Eros rides through the seas on the back of a Triton, a long shell slung over his left shoulder. Such quasi-mythological details belong to the so-called Pompeiian Third Style of mural decoration that flourished around the Bay of Naples at the height of the Julio-Claudian period.

PALMYRENE FUNERARY BUST. Limestone, ca. A.D. 100-150. H. 22 in. *Gift of the Estate of Dana Estes. 10.76*

This man in tunic and himation or outer robe lived in Palmyra in Syria, a noted caravan city inhabited by Greek, Arab, and other native merchants. The linear, dematerialized style of this portrait, with large eyes and carefully defined hair, anticipates late Roman art in the East.

A ROMAN STANDARD-BEARER. Fragment of an historical monument of the late first or early second centuries A.D. From Rome. H. 3¼ in. *Charles Amos Cummings Bequest Fund. 59.336*

This relief of a legionary in a bearskin cap has been linked with the arch commemorating the British victories of Claudius (A.D. 51). The arch may not have been finished until about A.D. 80. The soldier has a forceful face within the canon of Graeco-Roman ideal narrative sculpture.

ROMAN EMPEROR IN ARMOR. Marble, torso with head, arms, legs made separately. H. 43 in. *H. L. Pierce Fund. 99.346*

The statue was probably Domitian (reigned 81 to 96), for his favorite goddess Minerva is being honored on the breastplate. She stands on a cylindrical base flanked by two Victories in the pose and dress of dancers. This is an imitation in marble of an elaborate ceremonial cuirass in metal with stitched leather tabs and skirts below. Decoration on the shoulder strap and on the semicircular hinged plates (pteryges) on the bottom of the cuirass includes a stylized thunderbolt, ram's heads, lion's heads, winged Gorgoneions, a Pan's head, and an elephant's head. A tunic was worn beneath the cuirass. The right arm was raised, to hold a spear or scepter-staff.

GRIFFIN IN FOLIAGE. Section of Roman architectural relief in marble. Late first century A.D. H. 42 in. *Francis Bartlett Collection. 03.747*
The mythological beast from lands beyond the Black Sea stands in a riot of moldings and leaf ornament. The griffin's tail adds to the fantasy by turning into a huge scroll of acanthus leaves and stems. A second relief in the museum collection shows the griffin facing to the left. The two reliefs were probably placed over the doorway of a funerary structure or a public building.

SARCOPHAGUS. Deceased between two sets of the four seasons. Marble, Roman, ca. A.D. 275. L. 6 ft. 11 in. *Gift of A. Dexter. 92.2583*
The deceased is clad as a hunter with winter leggings. The sets of seasons, winter being closest to the deceased, dance with various attributes and animals connected with the harvests or the worship of Bacchus, god of the vineyards. Rough and ready decorative sculpture, this relief demonstrates the religious curiosities moving the Roman world on the eve of Christianity.

OVER LIFE-SIZED HEAD OF A MAN OF INTELLECT. Pentelic marble, Greek, ca. A.D. 375-400. H. 17 in. *J. H. and E. A. Payne Fund. 62.465*
Found years ago at Agia Paraskevi in the suburbs of Athens near the ruins of a large Early Christian basilica, this noble elder of late antiquity is a rare document of monumental Greek sculpture on the eve of the Byzantine Empire. He may be a Pagan or Christian philosopher and, from comparison with Early Christian reliefs, he may well be Saint Paul.

STATUETTE OF A GODDESS. Gold and Silver, Roman Imperial period, third or fourth century A.D. H. 8¼ in. *Theodora Wilbour Fund in memory of Charlotte Beebe Wilbour. 66.425*
The divinity may be Juno Sospita or a manifestation of Jupiter's consort worshipped in the empire's Celtic provinces. Semi-precious stones complete the effect of the silver with details (including three snakes within the chiton) in gold.

RIBBED GLASS BOWL. Blue and white glass, first century A.D.   D. 4¼ in. *H. L. Pierce Fund. 99.442*
The form and coloring of this bowl or offering dish (phiale) reflect similar vessels carved out of semi-precious stones. Ancient writers testify to the great value of these bowls, and a creation such as this in glass was an effort to give the art wider circulation at a reasonable price.

GLASS CUP. Translucent, very pale yellow glass.   D. 4½ in. Perhaps Syrian, first century A.D. *Bequest of Charles B. Hoyt. 50.2285*
The cup's shape, of traditional "skyphos" form, goes back through Hellenistic metalwork to Attic painted vases of the fifth and fourth centuries B.C.

MEDALLION OF MAXIMIANUS HERCULEUS. Gold, ca. A.D. 306.   D. 33 mm. *Theodora Wilbour Fund in memory of Zoë Wilbour. 59.497*
On the obverse the Emperor Maximianus wears the lion's skin of Hercules under whose protection he felt himself to be. The reverse shows Hercules standing, holding a bow in his left hand and a club in his right. Struck at the mint of Rome, the medallion was part of a hoard of aurei and gold medallions dating to the Tetrarch period. The portrait is a superlative example of the cubist style in the Roman Empire under Diocletian and his colleagues the Tetrarchs.

DEPARTMENT OF CONTEMPORARY ART

The Department of Contemporary Art was founded in September 1971. It is primarily responsible for paintings and sculpture by artists who have emerged since 1945, the period commencing with the revival of abstract painting and the ascendancy of the New York School. The first purchase of the department, Jackson Pollock's *Number 10,* formed the cornerstone of the collection. Under an acquisition policy that was based upon outstanding quality and consideration for works that are both characteristic and unique to the artists' sensibility, the permanent collection expanded to achieve national importance. Works by Bannard, Bush, Dzubas, Gottlieb, Goodnough, Hofmann, Motherwell, and Poons were among those added to a small but significant body of works previously owned by the museum. This was made possible by the Sophie M. Friedman, Charles H. Hayden, Edwin E. Jack, Otis Norcross, and Arthur G. Tompkins funds and the generous gifts of Mr. and Mrs. Charles R. Blyth, Dr. and Mrs. Henry Foster, Susan Morse Hilles, and Mr. Max Wasserman among others.

In December 1972 the department received the exciting gift and promised gifts of six major paintings by Morris Louis. Combined with three works that are already in the museum's collection, the group forms the largest and most comprehensive public collection of works by one of the world's greatest modern artists. A repository for archives containing letters and original documents related to Louis' achievement will also establish the museum as a study center for his work.

Works by younger artists and recent art have also been acquired through gifts and supplemented with purchases.

In addition to forming a permanent collection, it is the responsibility of the department to present what it considers to be the best in recent art. One-man and group shows organized by the department have received

CUBI XVIII, 1964. David Smith, American (1906-1965).   Polished stainless steel.
H. 9 ft. 7¾ in., w. of base 21¾ in; depth of base 20¾ in. *Anonymous Centennial
gift. 68.280*
Cubes and cylinders of burnished steel, counterbalanced in tangential relationship, create a feeling of expansion and extension into space. The calligraphically
polished surfaces reflect and relate the form to the surrounding atmosphere and
convey a sense of weightlessness.

TWILIGHT, 1957. Hans Hofmann, American, b. Germany (1880-1966). Oil on plywood. 48 x 36 in. *Gift of Dr. and Mrs. Henry L. Foster. 1973.171*
Twilight is a work from Hofmann's classic period of abstract expressionism. Executed entirely with palette knife, the work reveals Hofmann's highly individual sense for dense sculptural surface organization and his distinctive feeling for the expressive potentials of color.

international acclaim and have made Boston a center for fresh activity.

Through the generous gift of Dr. and Mrs. Henry Foster, the contemporary department acquired an additional large new gallery (to be completed in 1975) for the purpose of housing its permanent collection and especially the nine paintings of Morris Louis.

ZIG VIII, 1965. David Smith, American (1906-1965).   Polychromed steel.
H. 8 ft. 4¾ in., w. 7 ft. 7½ in.; depth 6 ft. 11 in. *Centennial Purchase Fund.*
68.279

In this monumental work from the Zig Series, Smith has freed sculpture from
the literalness of the pedestal by integrating it into the work and affixing wheels
to achieve a feeling of weightlessness and mobility. The zigzag I-beam piercing
the polychromed target creates a dynamic multidirectional movement and
vitalizes space in front of and behind the circular plane.

DELTA GAMMA. Morris Louis, American (1912-1962).   Acrylic on canvas. 103½ x 150⅝ in. *Anonymous gift. 1972.1074*
Delta Gamma is one of a series of unfurleds that Louis himself considered to be his greatest achievement and the culmination of his search for a format through which color could achieve new expressive eloquence. An astonishingly expansive feeling results from the dynamic composition in which the center of the canvas is emptied and rivulets of intense color are pushed to the margins.

BETH TET, 1958. Morris Louis, American (1912-1962).   Acrylic on canvas. 91½ x 133¼ in. *Anonymous gift. 1972.1072*
In *Beth Tet*, one of the most monumental works from his "veil series," Louis has put color into color by staining successive transparent layers of one hue over another into unprimed canvas. Despite the radiance of individual colors, the thin washes become muted and ambiguously shaded, and uniquely delicate and subtle fluctuations of tone and value emerge.

NUMBER 10, 1949. Jackson Pollock, American (1912-1956).   Oil on canvas. 18 x 107 in. *Arthur G. Tompkins and Sophie M. Friedman funds. 1971.638*
This painting from Pollock's classical drip period was executed at the height of the artist's career. It has exceptional clarity and variety of accent achieved by an interwoven network of black pigment, the light and atmospheric qualities of aluminum paint, and splashes of color.

OPEN IN OCHRE, 1967-1970. Robert Motherwell, American (b. 1915). Acrylic on canvas. 92 x 69 in. *Charles H. Hayden Fund. 1972.211*
A unique painting from Motherwell's open series, *Open in Ochre* achieves a remarkable feeling for scale and mastery of the interaction between line and plane. The dark somber color field is charged by the dynamic tension of strong black lines twisted off balance and stabilized by thin white lines and the framing edge.

ALKAHEST OF PARACELSUS, 1945. Adolph Gottlieb, American (1903-1974). Oil on canvas. 60¼ x 44 in. *Arthur G. Tompkins Fund. 1973.599*
From the emergent phase of American abstract painting, this work from Gottlieb's "pictograph series" (1940-1950) shows its roots in surrealism and cubism. A distinct kind of vitality is achieved through the compositional un-balancing of the grid structure, lively white linear calligraphy, and the rich tonal handling of earth colors and darker hues.

RAILROAD HORSE, 1971. Larry Poons, American (b. 1937). Acrylic on canvas. 94½ x 303 in. *Charles H. Hayden Fund. 1971.639*
Working in a highly original manner, Poons has poured pigment mixed with gel onto an upright canvas. Rich impressionist color nuances emerge without mixing and vie with the tactility of the surface.

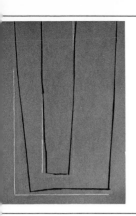

DEPARTMENT OF EGYPTIAN AND
ANCIENT NEAR EASTERN ART

The initial steps taken in the formation of the Department of Egyptian A
were the gifts in 1872 of the Way Collection of Antiquities and in 1875 c
several monumental sculptures from the Lowell Institute, collected in th
1830's by John Lowell of Boston, founder of the institute. During the suc
ceeding years the collections increased by occasional gifts from Sir Flinder
Petrie's excavations in Egypt and other sources, and by purchases. An es
pecially important gift was that of Theodore M. Davis of Newport, wh
presented the museum with a large group of objects from the Nev
Kingdom Tomb of Tuthmosis IV, excavated by Davis in the Valley of th
Kings. In 1905 the museum, mindful of the scientific and artistic value o
such an undertaking, joined with Harvard University to form an expeditio
in Egypt based at the Great Pyramids of Giza under the direction of Dr
George Andrew Reisner. During the forty-year duration of the Harvard
Boston Expedition at Giza the museum came into possession, through th
share of antiquities assigned the expedition by the Egyptian government, of a
collection of Old Kingdom sculpture unparalleled except at Cairo. Excava
tions under Dr. Reisner's leadership in the Sudan brought to the museum
important collections of Kushite art from the burials of Kushite royalty (80(
B.C.-A.D. 300) at Kurru, Nuri, and Meroë, and of Middle Kingdom from
Kerma near the Third Cataract of the Nile. Excavations elsewhere in Egypt,
such as at the Middle Kingdom site of Deir el-Bersheh, brought other im
portant material to the museum. The expedition was closed after World War
II, and since that time the department has depended on gifts and purchases
to add to its holdings. The entire range of Egyptian art is covered by the
collections in the museum, and although the Old Kingdom and Kushite art
from the Sudan are particularly well represented, the Middle Kingdom and
the New Kingdom and the Late Period hold a position that is second to the

ollections of few other institutions.

More recently in 1958 the department assumed charge of the "Art of the Ancient Near East," a small but distinguished collection of sculpture, bronzes, and other objects from Mesopotamia, the Syrian Coast, Anatolia, and Persia. The gifts from Mrs. Edward Jackson Holmes of Persian bronzes of the first millennium B.C. have provided the museum with one of the important collections of these objects.

One of the continuing programs of the department is the publication of the results of the expedition in the series *History of the Giza Necropolis* (published: vols. 1 and 2), *Giza Mastabas* (published: vol. 1), *The Reisner Papyri* (published: vols. 1-3), *Second Cataract Forts* (published: vols. 1 and 2), and *Royal Cemeteries of Kush* (published: vols. 1-5), and elsewhere. There are three handbooks of the collections: *Ancient Egypt* (4th ed., 1960), by William Stevenson Smith; *The Egyptian Department and Its Excavations* (1958), by Dows Dunham; and *Art of the Ancient Near East in Boston* (1962), by Edward L. B. Terrace.

Egypt

PAINTED BUST OF THE VIZIER ANKH-HAF. Limestone. Reign of Chephren, builder of the Second Pyramid at Giza, Dynasty IV, 2625-2600 B.C.   H. 21 in. *Harvard-Boston Expedition. 27.442*

The major achievement of the artists of the Fourth Dynasty was the development of portrait sculpture, and the bust of Ankh-haf delicately modeled in limestone is perhaps the finest portrait to survive from the Old Kingdom. The limestone has been augmented by plaster and then painted to give a portrait of this important official of the reign of Chephren. The subtle treatment of the hairline and facial muscles is unusual at this period. Ankh-haf's mastaba tomb is the largest in the area east of the pyramid of Cheops.

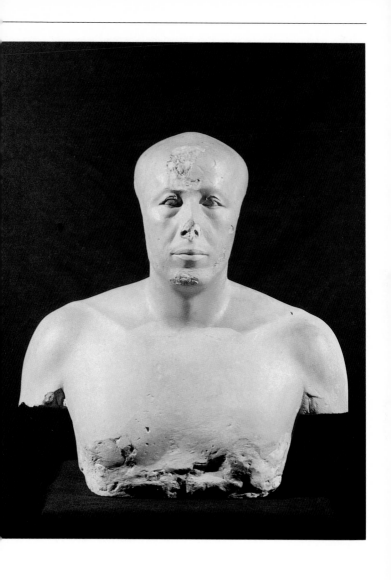

POTTERY BOWL, hippopotami painted in interior. From Mesaeed, Early Predynastic period, ca. 3500 B.C.   D. 7½ in. *Harvard-Boston Expedition. 11.312*
As in many early cultures, it is in the pottery that are found the first steps
toward a higher civilization in Egypt, and the decoration of this bowl already
shows the sophistication that becomes characteristic of Egyptian art. The linear
treatment suggests a basketry prototype.

SLATE PALETTE in form of a tortoise, with shell-inlay eye. From Naga-el-Hai.
Predynastic period, ca. 3400 B.C.   H. 6¼ in. *Harvard-Boston Expedition. 13.3492*
The slate palettes were used by the predynastic Egyptians to grind green
malachite for use as eye paint. The collection includes a large selection.

POTTERY HIPPOPOTAMUS. Early Predynastic period, ca. 3500 B.C.   L. 11½ in.
Gift of Mrs. Charles Gaston Smith's Group. 48.252

MASK from composite statue of a man. Wood. Said to be from the royal graves at Abydos, Dynasty 1, ca. 3000 B.C.   H. 6½ in. *Gift of J. J. Klejman. 60.1181*
Very few monuments of the earliest sculpture of dynastic Egypt are preserved, and this is one of the most significant of these. It appears to represent a foreigner, perhaps a Libyan prince captured by the Egyptians.

"RESERVE HEAD" OF A PRINCESS. White limestone. Reign of Cheops, builder of the Great Pyramid at Giza, Dynasty IV, 2656-2633 B.C.   H. 11¾ in. *Harvard-Boston Expedition. 14.719*
The "reserve heads" are a type of sculpture unparalleled at any other time of Egyptian history. They are realistic portraits of their owners, probably put in the tombs to replace the mummies should they be destroyed, hence their name. The heavy lips and high cheekbones are African features.

HEAD OF A KING in the White Crown of Upper Egypt. Indurated limestone. Perhap King Khasekhem, Dynasty II, ca. 2800 B.C.   H. 13½ in. *Edwin E. Jack Fund. 58.324*
The sharply modeled eyes and distinct eyebrow ridge resemble the features of the statues of King Khasekhem from Hierakonpolis.

RELIEF OF THE NOBLE NOFER (detail). From Giza, Dynasty IV, ca. 2640 B.C.
H. of complete relief 37½ in. *Harvard-Boston Expedition. 07.1002*
The unusual acquiline nose is clearly rendered in the reserve head of the same
official shown to the right.

"RESERVE HEAD" OF NOFER. White limestone. From mastaba of Nofer at
Giza, Dynasty IV, ca. 2640 B.C. H. 10⅝ in. *Harvard-Boston Expedition. 06.1886*
The strong features of the face correspond to those of the relief to the left. This
is one of the few cases where relief and sculpture of the same person show a
close resemblance.

COLOSSAL STATUE OF MYCERINUS, builder of the Third Pyramid at Giza
(detail). Alabaster. Dynasty IV, 2599-2571 B.C. H. of complete statue 6 ft. 11 in.
Harvard-Boston Expedition. 09.204
This great statue is one of the largest sculptures from the Old Kingdom. A
mustache and indication of a chin beard in ink are visible in this photograph
taken soon after its discovery and before the head was fitted to the fragments
of the torso and body. Waxy, translucent alabaster was one of the favorite
materials of the sculptor at all periods, and objects as small as tiny vases and as
huge as this colossal statue of Mycerinus were made in it. This is one of the
largest, nearly intact, sculptures from the Old Kingdom and once adorned the
temple of Mycerinus' pyramid at Giza. The statue is strangely proportioned:
the very broad shoulders suggest that they were enlarged to give a correct
impression when the statue is seen from below, but the tiny head is difficult
to understand. There is no doubt, however, that the head belongs to the
statue, since there is an exact fit with part of the shoulders. The headdress is the
so-called lappet-wig representing pleated linen. A particular feature of this fine
statue is the facile, naturalistic treatment of the knee structure.

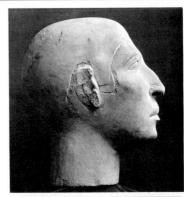

TRIAD: personification of the Hare Nome of Upper Egypt, the goddess Hathor, Mycerinus (detail). Slate schist. From Giza, Dynasty IV, 2599-2571 B.C. H. 33 in. *Harvard-Boston Expedition. 09.200*

Personifying the various nomes or provinces into which Egypt was divided for administrative purposes (probably representing very much earlier separate and independent areas), the nome triads of Mycerinus are among the most interesting sculptural inventions of the Fourth Dynasty. Carved by the best sculptors of the court, they are in fact some of the greatest works of art from Egypt. The purpose of the triads was evidently to represent in the temple the offerings of various sorts that might be brought from the separate nomes. Hathor, goddess of fertility, is associated with the king and nome in these triads. She is represented in female form, but with the sun disk and cow's horns indicating her original form as a cow goddess.

PAIR STATUE OF MYCERINUS AND HIS QUEEN, KHA-MERER-NEBTY II (detail). Slate schist. From Giza, Dynasty IV, 2599-2571 B.C.   H. of complete statue 54½ in. *Harvard-Boston Expedition. 11.1738*

The first "pair statue" is this royal group, which set a standard to be followed throughout the remainder of Egyptian history. Perhaps in more than any other statue, a serious nobility is expressed to a consummate degree as the queen clasps her royal husband and they face eternity together. The dignity and grandeur of this, one of the most famous statues from Egypt, are in keeping with the intimacy of the subject. The king and queen are shown in close embrace, the queen extending her arm around her spouse and lightly touching his left arm. This double statue is the first dated example of what was to become one of the popular types of Egyptian sculpture. The calm, straightforward gaze of their eyes reflects the easy confidence of this period of Egyptian history. The nobility of their stance is intensified by the powerful modulation of muscle and bone structure.

CYLINDER SEAL. Gold. From Aegean or Western Asia, Dynasty V, 2490-2450 B.C.
H. 2⅝ in. *Centennial Gift of Landon T. Clay. 68.115*
This extraordinary seal bears the names of two rulers of late Dynasty V. The
finely cut hieroglyphs are exceptional. The seal is said to have been found with
a hoard of gold jewelry also in the museum.

PORTRAIT OF A YOUNG KING, perhaps Mycerinus or Shepseskaf. Alabaster.
From Giza, Dynasty IV, 2599-2567 B.C.   H. 11¼ in. *Harvard-Boston Expedition.*
09.203

MASK FROM A MUMMY. Plaster. From Giza, Dynasty VI, ca. 2400 B.C.
H. 8¼ in. *Harvard-Boston Expedition. 39.828*
This rare example of an Old Kingdom mummy mask shows a sensitive modeling
reminiscent of the earlier reserve heads. Giza mastaba G 2037 b X.

PORTRAIT OF AN OFFICIAL NAMED SESHEM-NOFER. Red granite. from Giza,
Dynasty IV, 2571-2567 B.C.   H. 9¾ in. *Harvard-Boston Expedition. 12.1487*

STATUETTE OF A WOMAN TENDING A FIRE. Painted limestone. From Giza, Dynasty V, ca. 2500 B.C.   H. 9½ in. *Harvard-Boston Expedition. 21.2600*
The stone servant models of the Old Kingdom show the facility of the Egyptian craftsman, but in the Middle Kingdom both undistinguished and superb models were carved in wood. By the New Kingdom the models were completely replaced by the shawabti, a mummiform funerary figure.

SEATED STATUE OF PRINCE KHUENRE. Yellow limestone. From Giza, Dynasty IV, 2599-2571 B.C.   H. 12 in. *Harvard-Boston Expedition. 13.3140*
The rotund and slightly asymmetrical features of the face of this son of King Mycerinus give him an appearance of indolence. The slight swelling above the upper eyelid continues a stylistic tradition seen in his father's sculpture yet moderated in this softer stone. He sits in the characteristic position of a scribe.

DETAIL OF AGRICULTURAL SCENE FROM MASTABA OF PTAH-SEKHEM-ANKH. From Saqqarah, Dynasty V, ca. 2500 B.C. *Emily Esther Sears Fund. 04.1760*

STATUE OF METHETHY (detail). Painted wood. Said to be from Saqqarah, early Dynasty VI, ca. 2400 B.C.   H. of statue 31½ in. *Arthur Tracy Cabot Fund. 47.1455*

STATUE OF THE VIZIER MEHY. Wood. From Giza, reign of Unas, Dynasty V, 2450-2420 B.C.   H. 41½ in. *Harvard-Boston Expedition. 13.3466*

Whereas the Egyptian sculptor was reluctant to show arms and legs in free space in stone sculpture, he felt free to so treat wooden sculpture. The nude statue of the Vizier Mehy shows him with the left arm extended in which he once held a staff of office, as shown in the relief of Nofer. The high quality of this sculpture makes it one of the most important of its kind from the Old Kingdom. It is interesting to compare it with the wooden mask of the First Dynasty, which already shows the type to be represented four or five hundred years later as in this statue of Mehy.

OFFERING BEARERS FROM THE TOMB OF DJEHUTY-NEKHT. Painted wood. From Bersheh in Upper Egypt, Dynasty XII, ca. 1860 B.C.   L. 21 in. *Harvard-Boston Expedition. 21.326*
The tomb of Djehuty-Nekht at Bersheh is one of the most important excavated by the museum's expedition. From it came the miraculously preserved painted coffin of Djehuty-Nekht, as well as an interesting series of crudely but vivaciously made model figures. Also from this great tomb comes the astonishing procession of offering bearers, one of the finest of its kind to be preserved. The procession is led by a priest, who carries over his shoulder a sacred vessel and in his hand a fan or mirror case. He leads three female bearers, two of whom support chests of offerings on their heads and carry live ducks in their right hands. The tall, graceful forms of the figures are characteristic of the period.

STATUE OF WEPWAWET-EM-HAT. Painted wood. From Assiut, end of First Intermediate Period, ca. 2100 B.C.   H. 43¾ in. *Emily Esther Sears Fund. 04.1780*
In the breakdown of the Egyptian government and civilization that followed the end of the Old Kingdom, many local centers were left to create their own styles in sculpture and the other arts. Assiut was one of the important towns during this Intermediate Period, which lasted for about 200 years before the foundation of the Middle Kingdom. This statue, dating near the end of the Intermediate Period, represents an official named Wepwawet-em-hat. While the sculpture is better preserved than that of Mehy and retains the long staff and the *sekhem-wand*, the style is in considerable contrast to that of Mehy. No longer is subtle modeling indicated, but rather conventional and highly stylized forms are employed, such as in the angular treatment of the face. Note, however, that the traditional type of the standing man is still used.

COFFIN OF DJEHUTY-NEKHT (detail). Painted cedar wood. From Bersheh in Upper Egypt, Dynasty XII, ca. 1860 B.C.   Total h. of panel 44 in. *Harvard-Boston Expedition. 20.1822*
Easel painting was unknown in ancient Egypt but the paintings on the side of the Bersheh coffin are similar in conception and execution. They were painted on a small scale with a free brush technique, with which the artist portrayed the most subtle shading and exquisite detail.

RELIEF OF TWO FEMALE BEARERS CARRYING A JAR. Limestone. From the chapel of the tomb of Queen Nofru at Deir el Bahri. Dynasty XI, ca. 2050 B.C. W. 12¾ in. *J. H. and E. A. Payne Fund. 1973.147*
The gem-like precision illustrated by the master sculptors of Dynasty XI is evident in the treatment of the hair and the rope.

TILES IN FORM OF LION, CAVETTO MOLDING, AND EARLY PALMETTES. Blue faience. From Kerma in the Sudan, ca. 1800 B.C.   L. of lion 46 in. *Harvard-Boston Expedition. 20.1224*
Faience architectural ornament is known from the earliest periods of dynastic history, but at Kerma, far to the south in the Sudan, the Middle Kingdom Egyptian settlers invented the use of large-scale figures made of faience for the façades of tomb chapels. Not even in Egypt were such large faience figures ever used.

OVERLAYS ON A CONJECTURALLY RESTORED CAP. Mica. From Kerma in the Sudan, ca. 1800 B.C. H. 5¼ in. *Harvard-Boston Expedition. 20.1768*

MIRROR. Bronze. From Semna at the Second Cataract, New Kingdom, ca. 1400 B.C. H. 8¾ in. *Harvard-Boston Expedition. 29.1197*
The New Kingdom signals Egypt's arrival as a world power, and one pharaoh after another attempted to establish Egyptian sovereignty over outlying lands, especially in Syria, a source of constant irritation in the past. Egyptian art takes on new forms; there are new materials; the scope of pictorial imagery broadens. Copper and bronze had been used for utilitarian and decorative purposes from a very early period. Few bronzes are prettier than this charming mirror with a handle in the form of a graceful unclothed girl holding in outstretched hands the tips of a beautifully stylized papyrus flower.

STATUE OF THE LADY SENNUWY. Black granite. From Kerma in the Sudan, Dynasty XII, ca. 1950 B.C. H. of complete figure 67½ in. *Harvard-Boston Expedition. 14.720*
The Middle Kingdom sculptor found a completely new interest in the psychology of his subjects, which is revealed in certain royal and private portraits. In contrast, the simple grandeur and noble reserve of the Lady Sennuwy hark back to the ancient traditions of idealism. During the Middle Kingdom, in Dynasty XII, there are two strong trends in sculpture. One, represented by the magnificent statue of the Lady Sennuwy, recalls the Memphite traditions of the Old Kingdom in its simplicity of form and directness of approach. She sits confidently and restfully, holding a lotus flower in her hand, and gazes out with a certain serenity and reserve. The statue was found far to the south, at Kerma in the Sudan, where the Egyptians had a trading fort during the Middle Kingdom. The cracks covering the surface of the stone are the result of an ancient fire in her tomb.

FRAGMENT OF COLUMN DRUM. From Amarna/Hermopolis. Dynasty XVIII, 1372-1355 B.C.   H. 8⅝ in. *Edward J. and Mary S. Holmes Fund. 67.637*
The palaces and temples of the reign were constructed of small blocks in the manner of brickwork. When the buildings were dismantled by Akhenaten's successors, the thousands of blocks separated from their compositional context become like fragments in a puzzle with heads and bodies rarely on the same block. The Boston section of a column drum shows the king on the right followed by Nefertiti, who holds a libation vessel aloft, and the princess Meritaten bearing a sistrum. Behind the latter is a representation of the same princess from a similar scene, facing in the opposite direction. Among the features of Amarna art represented are the long neck and exaggerated hips of the queen, the curiously shaped head of the princess, and the sun's rays ending in hands radiating from the right toward the royal family.

RELIEF OF AKHENATEN AS A SPHINX. Limestone. From Amarna/Hermopolis, Dynasty XVIII, 1372-1355 B.C.   H. 20 in. *Egyptian Curator's Fund. 64.1944*
The sphinx presents the cartouches of the Aten to the sun disk and receives the emblems of life.

HEAD OF AMENHOTEP II. Limestone. From Hu in Upper Egypt. Dynasty XVIII, 1450-1423 B.C.   H. 5 in. *Gift of Egypt Exploration Fund. 99.733*

HEAD OF A KING, PERHAPS TUTANKHAMON. Sandstone. Dynasty XVIII, ca. 1350 B.C.   H. 11¾ in. *Gift of Miss Mary Ames. 11.1533*

HEAD OF AMENHOTEP III. Quartzite. Dynasty XVIII, 1410-1372 B.C.   H. 20½ in.
Gift of Miss Anna D. Slocum. 09.288
The almost exotic flavor of the almond eyes and sensuous mouth of this head of
Amenhotep III was achieved by the sculptors of an imperial court that was
showing signs of degeneration, and in the sculpture of the period one can sense
the soft, luxurious life of the height of the 18th Dynasty.

FRAGMENT SHOWING QUEEN NEFERTITI ADORING THE ATEN SUN-DISK.
Alabaster. From Amarna, Dynasty XVIII, 1372-1355 B.C.   H. 6½ in. *Gift of Egypt
Exploration Society through the Hon. Robert Bass. 37.3*
The exaggerated, almost grotesque, form of Akhenaten's Queen is typical of the
new experiments in art during the reign of the "heretic of Amarna."

RELIEF SHOWING THE NILE GOD HAPI. Limestone. From a throne of King Ay.
Dynasty XVIII, ca. 1345 B.C.   H. 18 in. *Gift of Edward Waldo Forbes. 50.3789*
The Nile god Hapi was represented as a male with the breasts of a female,
because the god represented the fecundity of the river that was the life blood
of Egypt. He is usually represented in two aspects, one, as here, wearing the
papyrus plant of Lower Egypt, and the other, the lily plant of Upper Egypt. The
two aspects are often shown facing each other, tying together the plants of
Upper and Lower Egypt.

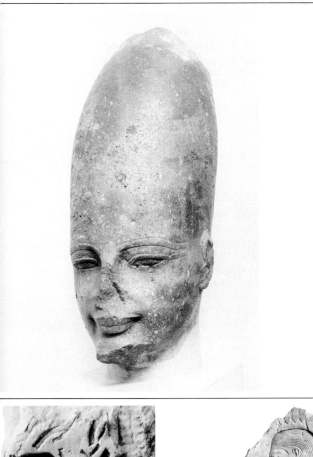

RELIEF OF THE CUP-BEARER TJA-WY (detail). Limestone. Probably from Memphis. Dynasty XVIII, reign of Amenhotep III, 1410-1372 B.C.   H. of entire relief 29 in. *Edward J. and Mary S. Holmes Fund. 1972.651*
Tja-wy with his mother and father is offered a bowl of food or drink by his sister to the accompaniment of the family musicians.

INLAY OF HEAD OF A KING, PERHAPS SETI I. Red jasper. Dynasty XIX, 1313-1301 B.C.   H. 1 in. *Harriet Otis Cruft Fund. 40.72*
Egyptian jewelry was made with precious metals, semi-precious stones, glass, faience, and other materials. Often several materials were used together to make up colorful objects of various kinds. The red jasper head, brilliantly polished, comes from such a composite object, perhaps the decoration of a jeweled box. Although it is impossible to reconstruct the exact form of the original, it might have included a blue glass or lapis crown, a white glass or faience gown, and other materials. Red jasper was chosen for the face because it was the conventional color for the skin of a man.

STATUE OF A PRIEST FROM MESHEIKH IN UPPER EGYPT. Wood. Late New Kingdom, ca. 12th century B.C.   H. 20¼ in. *Harvard-Boston Expedition. 12.1240*

STATUETTE OF KHONSU-IR-AA. Diorite. End of Dynasty XXV, 670-660 B.C. H. 17 in. *James Fund. 07.494*

CAT ON A PAPYRUS COLUMN. Bronze. Late Period, 7th-6th century B.C. H. 19 in. *Martha A. Willcomb Fund. 52.1026*

RELIEF: PORTRAIT OF THE OWNER (detail). Limestone. Probably from the region of Memphis, Dynasty XXVI, ca. 535 B.C. H. 13½ in. *Otis Norcross Fund. 49.5*

STATUE OF KING ASPELTA (detail). Black granite. Complete height 10 ft. 9 in. From Gebel Barkal in the Sudan, Kushite, 6th century B.C. *Harvard-Boston Expedition. 23.730*

Although the Egyptians from the earliest periods had taken an interest in the Sudan far to the south beyond the first and second cataracts of the Nile, it was not until the Late Period that the natives of these southern regions took on the explicit characteristics of Egyptian civilization for their own. Finally the southerners invaded and conquered Egypt itself, ruling there as the twenty-fifth Dynasty. Returning to the south after their expulsion, their civilization resembled, in many respects, that of the north. The style of sculpture was derived directly from that of Egypt, but local characteristics are evident, especially in the form of the facial type, which is negroid. The heaviness and powerful muscle structure of these statues seem to reflect the strong-minded inhabitants of the south and must have recalled to them the days when they ruled Egypt itself. The roughened areas of the armlets, bracelets, anklets, sandals, kilt, and crown were left unpolished to take gold leaf, which was pressed into these areas.

CIRCULAR COSMETIC CONTAINER WITH FROG ON LID. Green faience. Anatolia (?), Dynasty 26, 664-525 B.C., or later. H. 1⅛in. *Edward J. and Mary S. Holmes Fund. 1970.571*
Said to have been found in Anatolia, this box with four compartments may have been a wedding gift for a noble lady. Egypt exported luxury wares to the Mediterranean world at this time. The frog on the lid guards the contents with its legs alert and ready to spring.

VULTURE HEAD. Ptolemaic, ca. 2nd century B.C. H. ⅞ in. *Gift of Mrs. Horace L. Mayer. 1971.748*
The vulture head is cast in solid gold with details finely carved with an engraving tool. It may have belonged to the crown of a queen or a statue of a royal personage or deity.

PECTORAL IN FORM OF WINGED ISIS. Gold. From Nuri in the Sudan, Kushite, tomb of King Amani-nataki-lebte, 538-520 B.C. L. 6½ in. *Harvard-Boston Expedition. 20.276*

PORTRAIT OF A MAN: THE "BOSTON GREEN HEAD." Green schist. From Saqqarah, 4th century B.C. H. 4¼ in. *Pierce Fund. 04.1749*
The Boston Green Head is justly famous as one of the finest works of art from Egypt. Two suggestions have been made about its date, one that it belongs to the fourth century B.C. and another that it should be placed in the second century B.C. Whichever is correct, the dispute does not in any way detract from the magnificent originality of this portrait of an aged man. Every effort has been made to portray the features of the real man: the wart under the left eye, the puckered skin over the brows, the raised eyebrows, the furrows along the cheeks, the grimly set mouth, the wrinkles at the corners of the eyes.

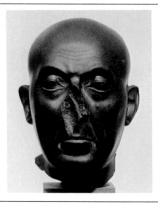

MUMMY PORTRAIT. Tempera on wood. Second century A.D.   H. ca. 17¼ in. *Gift of Egypt Exploration Fund. 02.825*

MASK FROM A MUMMY. Painted plaster. Second century A.D.   H. 8 in. *Samuel Putnam Avery Fund. 58.1196*

The Ancient Near East

WARRIOR WITH SILVER HELMET. Bronze. From Tell Judeideh in North Syria, ca. 2900 B.C.   H. 7 in. *Marriner Memorial Syrian Expedition. 49.118*
This and its companions found in the same deposit are the first true bronzes known.

IMPRESSION OF A CYLINDER SEAL: FIGURES AND ANIMALS IN LANDSCAPE. From Mesopotamia, Akkadian, ca. 2200 B.C. Diorite.   H. 1½ in. *Harriet Otis Cruft Fund. 34.199*
Although his subjects were usually hieratic and conventional, the artist of the cylinder seal occasionally achieved remarkable freedom and monumentality, as he did on this extraordinary landscape seal.

FRAGMENT OF VICTORY STELE (detail). Alabaster. From Mesopotamia, Akkadian ca. reign of Naram-Sin, 2230-2194 B.C.   H. of fragment 13¾ in. *Gift of the Guide Foundation through Dr. and Mrs. Edmundo Lassalle. 66.893*
The theme of enemy prisoners brought by officers and soldiers before the conqueror is one of the oldest and longest lasting in the representational arts of the ancient Near East. The Boston fragment of an Akkadian stele exhibits a gem-like workmanship in its treatment of the helmeted and bearded warrior following a file of bound captives. Note the contrast between the subtly modeled face, arms, and torso and the minute details of the mustache, beard, and fingernail, as well as the fittings of the hafted axe.

STELE SHOWING A FEMALE FIGURE SEATED AT A TABLE OF OFFERINGS. Basalt. From Marash in southeastern Turkey, Neo-Hittite, 9th-8th century B.C.   H. 18 in. *Helen and Alice Colburn Fund and gift of Horace L. Mayer. 60.1156*

RELIEF: HEAD OF WINGED FIGURE (detail). Limestone. From Nimrud in Assyria, reign of Ashurnasirpal II, 883-859 B.C.   H. of complete relief, 7 ft. 5 in. *Charles Amos Cummings Bequest Fund. 33.731*

RELIEF: BABYLONIANS BEING LED INTO CAPTIVITY BY ASSYRIANS (detail).
Limestone. From Nineveh (Kuyunjik) in Assyria, reign of Sennacherib, 760-681
B.C. H. of complete relief 26 in. *Charles Amos Cummings Bequest Fund and gift
of Horace L. Mayer. 60.133*

Narrative art in the Assyrian palace reliefs was developed to illustrate the ritual
activities of the kings and their widespread and recurrent military campaigns.
These latter compositions, with their imposing sweep and topographical details,
are best illustrated in the extensive series from several reigns that form part of
the marvels brought to the British Museum by Sir Henry Austen Layard, an
extraordinary man who numbered Disraeli among his friends. The two Boston
reliefs are from the North Palace of Sennacherib at Nineveh. One depicts the
forced march of Babylonian women from their native palm groves to a distant
exile. A mother is shown holding a leather water skin to her child.

IMPRESSION OF CYLINDER SEAL: PRIEST BEFORE TWO ALTARS. Chalcedony.
From Mesopotamia, Neo-Babylonian, 7th-6th century B.C. H. 1½ in. *Seth K.
Sweetser Fund. 41.478*

BUST OF DEDICANT OR GODDESS. Terracotta. From Mesopotamia, Syria, or
Iran, 1900-1700 B.C. H. 15 in., w. 18 in. *Edward J. and Mary S. Holmes Fund.
1972.870*

MOUNTAIN SHEEP. Silver. From Iran, Achaemenian, 6th-5th centuries B.C.
L. 2¾ in. *J. H. and E. A. Payne Fund. 59.14*
There are few objects in the collection so appealing and irresistible as the little
mountain sheep, the head and horns of which were separately made and
attached. Three of the legs are three-dimensional, while the fourth, tucked
underneath, is incised. Although certainly Achaemenian in origin, it was
acquired from a collector in Bombay.

RELIEF OF LION ATTACKING BULL. Limestone. From Palace H at Persepolis in
Persia, Achaemenian, 5th century B.C.   L. 5 ft. 9 in. *Permanent loan from
Oriental Institute, University of Chicago. 36.37*
Although repeated in apparently endless numbers, the sculptures of the
imperial buildings of the Achaemenian court at Persepolis are remarkable for
their superb carving. The theme of the lion attacking a bull was an ancient one
in the Near East before it was so powerfully portrayed by the Achaemenians.

HEAD FROM STATUE OF PARTHIAN NOBLE. Limestone. From Iraq or Iran, 2nd
century A.D.   H. 9½ in. *Edwin E. Jack Fund. 1971.345*
Although perhaps not a true portrait, this impressive sculpture shows many of
the features of Parthian art, which is essentially a provincial version of Roman
sculpture.

DEPARTMENT OF EUROPEAN DECORATIVE ARTS AND SCULPTURE

The history of this department officially began in 1908 when appropriate sections of the museum collections were organized under the title of "Department of Western Art." Though the collections at the end of the nineteenth century consisted largely of plaster casts, the latter years of the century also saw the arrival of the Wales collection of European ceramics, significant examples of Italian Renaissance sculpture, and the extraordinary carved and gilt panels designed by Ledoux for the Hotel Montmorency in Paris.

In 1928 a new wing in the present building was inaugurated to accommodate the growing collections and the name of the department was changed to "Department of Decorative Arts of Europe and America" to reflect the scope of those collections. In 1971 the American collections were organized within a separate department, leaving the Department of European Decorative Arts as an independent unit.

Mr. Edwin J. Hipkiss, the department's first curator, and a succession of gifted curatorial staff contributed greatly to bringing distinctive shape, quality, and great interest to the department's collections. Georg Swarzenski as Research Fellow and his son, Hanns Swarzenski, curator for fifteen years, broadened the department's collections, strengthening especially the medieval field and baroque sculpture and decorative arts, at the same time forming specialized sections of the collections such as sculptor's models, or "bozzettis."

At this time, the department is concerned chiefly with the decorative arts and sculpture of Europe in the broadest sense, from the sixth century until 1944. The museum's collection of Chinese export porcelain remains this department's responsibility, as does the Leslie Lindsay Mason Collection of Musical Instruments, from which springs a dynamic program of performance and instruction in the history, use, and construction of ancient musical instruments.

In addition to strength in the medieval collection, the Department of European Decorative Arts and Sculpture offers to its public a relatively comprehensive collection of English silver from the fifteenth century into the nineteenth, and a distinguished collection of French decorative arts of the eighteenth century, including the bequest of Forsyth Wickes, which has served to complement the Swan Collection of eighteenth century French furniture since 1965. English porcelain of the eighteenth century has become a special interest of the department due to the arrival of the Katz Collection, which, added to earlier acquisitions (notably the Paine collection), makes the Museum of Fine Arts a major international resource for the study and enjoyment of this field.

New directions are currently being pursued, particularly as regards nineteenth century sculpture and decorative arts and English furniture of the eighteenth and nineteenth centuries, of interest for itself and for the study of the museum's holdings of American furniture. Further, it is hoped that a strong collection of English furniture will complement an already distinguished collection of English silver and porcelain.

VIRGIN AND CHILD. Polychromed and gilded oak.   H. 61 in. Île-de-France, early 13th century. *William F. Warden Fund. 57.701*
The highly developed drapery style of the statue with its undulating, deep-cut folds is characteristic of Early Gothic cathedral sculpture of Northern France, but only in the works of the greatest masters of the period does one meet such understanding for the organic function of the body and such grace, gentleness, and serenity.

OLIPHANT. Ivory. South Italy (Salerno?), late 11th century. H. 21 in. *Frederick Brown Fund and H. E. Bolles Fund. 57.581*
Carved from elephant tusks, oliphants were used in the Middle Ages as hunting and signal horns as well as for drinking vessels. This magnificent example served the latter purpose and was most likely a "tenure horn" symbolizing the legal transfer of land. The fantastic beasts, plants, and mythological subjects depicted on these horns are derived from Byzantine and late classical art and iconography

THE EMLY (or MONSEL of TERVOS) SHRINE. Silver inlay, gold, cloisonné enamel and gilt bronze on yew wood. Irish, ca. 800. H. 3½ in. *Theodora Wilbour Fund in memory of Charlotte Beebe Wilbour. 52.1396*
One of the rare surviving documents of Pre-Carolingian Anglo-Irish culture. Reliquary shrines of this kind were suspended on a strap and worn like a pendant. The style and technique used on the shrine recall the decorative taste of wandering peoples of the early middle ages. The animal head terminals on the top of the shrine seem specifically Nordic in their form.

PLAQUE DEPICTING THE CRUCIFIXION. Ivory. Paris, ca. 1300. H. 6¾ in., w. 4¼ in. *Gift of John Goelet in honor of Hanns Swarzenski. 1973.690*
This lovely relief of the crucified Christ, the Virgin, and St. John attended by angels typifies the mixture of deep religious feeling, graceful form, and courtly spirit that characterizes Gothic art of the fourteenth century, particularly in France. Hallmarks of the style are the elegant folds of the drapery, the unmistakable curve of the figures, the principals enclosed in an architectural setting. We may perhaps look to Paris, the focus of this courtly style of the early fourteenth century, for the origin of our ivory, possibly part of a three-part devotional piece called a triptych.

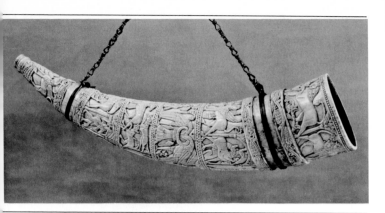

LITURGICAL FAN. Vellum painted on both sides with a floral design. Ivory handle incrusted with mother-of-pearl and nielloed silver. South Italy, late 12th century. Diam. 13 in.; handle, h. 12¼ in. *Gift of the Class of the Museum. 56.882*
Called *flabella*, such fans were carried by deacons during mass to chase flies from the chalice. Only a few examples have survived.

THE SONG OF THE THREE WORTHIES. Champlevé enamel on gilded copper. Mosan (Maastricht?), ca. 1150. H. 8⅛ in. *William F. Warden Fund. 51.7*
The three Hebrews in the fiery furnace are comforted by the approaching Angel of the Lord. The plaque's peculiar, slightly curved shape and the inscription along its semicircular border, referring to the Immaculate Birth of the Virgin, suggest that it formed part of a large ensemble. Another plaque of related shape and identical style, illustrating the Fleece of Gideon, survives in the museum in Lille, France, and may have been a part of the same complex.

THE CRUCIFIED CHRIST. Polychromed wood. Salzburg, late 11th century. H. 71 in. *Purchase fund. 51.1405*
Monumental crucifixes were placed over the high altars of Romanesque churches, but few have survived from the eleventh century that retain their original polychromy. In this moving figure, the sculptor has reduced the body to essential elements basic to the powerful expressive effect of the figure. Especially moving is the way in which the sculptor carved the head of Christ, as it falls upon the chest, the hair falling limply in large units that contribute equally to the formal and expressive statement of the figure.

THE VIRGIN. Gilt bronze. Eastern France, second half of 12th century. H. 6⅛ in. *William F. Warden Fund. 49.466*
The Virgin is the survivor of a Crucifixion group from which the Christ and the figure of St. John are lost. The elongated figure, the broadly conceived details, the drapery, which organizes the figure and contributes powerfully to the decorative effect, are all features of the Romanesque style.

MADONNA AND CHILD. Polychromed stone. Lombardy, late 12th century.
H. 29 in. *Maria Antoinette Evans Fund. 57.583*
This representation of the Madonna and Child assumes the Byzantine formula called "glykophilousa" ("sweetly loving Mother of God"). In the tender relationship of the figures, our group departs from the hieratic, frontal depiction of the theme commonly found in Romanesque art. Unusual is the finishing of the back of the piece, where the sculptor shows masterful resolution of formal problems.

BAPTISM OF CHRIST. Champlevé enamel and gilded copper. Limoges, first half of 13th century. H. 14½ in. *Francis Bartlett Fund. 50.858*
Originally forming part of an altar-frontal or retable, this applied relief is distinguished by a monumental nobility and formal clarity exceptional in the wholesale production of Limoges. The monochrome enamel of greyish-white, deliberately confined to the water, contrasts with the modeling effects of light and shadow on the shiny surface of the human figures embossed in gilded copper.

AQUAMANILE: SAMSON AND THE LION. Bronze, engraved. Lorraine or Upper Rhine, 13th century. H. 12 in. *Benjamin Shelton Fund. 40.233*
Pouring vessels of this type used for washing the hands were not uncommon in medieval times. This example, for centuries preserved in the church of Achern in the Black Forest, is an independent masterpiece. Were it not for the opening on Samson's head and the small dragonhead spout beneath the lion's left ear, one would not be aware that it had a practical purpose.

CROWNED HEAD. Marble. Pisa. Manner of Nicolo Pisano, ca. 1260-1280.
H. 4⅛ in. *Charles A. Cummings Fund. 47.1447*
An insistent use of the drill that suggests hair and beard while communicating a
surface energy and nervousness and the strong emotional effect of the eyes and
mouth link this head to late Roman antecedents and, because of the individual
character of that relationship, to the circle of Nicolo Pisano, who drew so
heavily on the art of late antiquity. This small head from an unknown relief may
have been part of a group of the Adoration of the Magi.

DEACON AND ACOLYTES. Nicolo Pisano in collaboration with Arnolfo di
Cambio and Fra Guglielmo, 1264-1267. Marble. Pisa.   H. 40⅛ in. *Grace M.
Edwards Fund. 47.1290*
With its companion in the National Museum, Florence, this pillar originally
supported the Tomb of St. Dominick in Bologna before this famous monument
— a masterpiece of Tuscan Proto-Renaissance — was "modernized" in the
Quattrocento by Nicolo dell'Arca. Each cleric carries an object for the service;
one, in a deacon's dress, holds the cushion that supports the missal on the altar.

THE HOLY TRINITY. Polychromed alabaster. Nottingham, England, first half of 15th century. H. 38½ in. *Decorative Arts Special Fund. 27.852*
As "Abraham representing Paradise," God the Father enfolds in his bosom nine human souls, among them a bishop and a king. Carved on the base are two kneeling donors in prayer. The Boston "Trinity" is, because of its quality of carving and finishing, an important document for the history of English medieval alabaster reliefs, which were produced in great numbers and whose quality was very often just routine.

THE BURIAL, OFFICE OF THE DEAD. Parchment. Paris, ca. 1400. Frame: h. 12½ in., w. 9 in. *Gift of Mr. John Goelet in honor of Hanns Swarzenski. 1973.691*
Set in a diminutive architectural setting, three monks chant over the deceased while two hooded *pleurants,* or "mourners," attend the coffin. Typical of French manuscript decoration of the period are *drôleries,* or grotesques, which inhabit the vine scrolls that enclose the scene. The religious and secular spirits coincide in this page in the inclusion of a wild life scene beneath the sober composition above.

SPOON: THE FOX IN A MONK'S DRESS PREACHING TO THE GEESE. Silver and enamel. Flanders or Burgundy, early 15th century.   H. 6⅞ in. *Helen and Alice Colburn Fund. 51.2472*
The spoon of silver and painted enamel is a rare surviving example of the luxurious taste of the Franco-Flemish court of the early fifteenth century. The bowl of the spoon depicts the fox preaching to the geese, an obvious satirical allusion to the church, which was popularized in contemporary manuscripts of the period. The reverse of the bowl is decorated with trees whose style recalls that found in the "Très Riches Heures" of the Duc de Berry.

JEWEL CASKET. Silver and tortoise shell. England, mid 15th century.   H. 2⅛ in., l. 3¼ in. *Arthur Mason Knapp Fund. 53.2375*
Made of precious and exotic materials, the little jewel casket draws upon architectural ornament for its decoration. Gothic tracery with delicate openwork and elaborate buttresses on the corners indicate the taste of the period and something of the insistent penetration of architectural forms into the decorative arts of the Middle Ages. The letters contained within the tracery panels would appear to be an abbreviated dedication.

LECTERN (detail). Brass. Belgium, 16th century.   H. 61 in. *Charles A. Cummings Fund. 48.256*
Cast in separate pieces, such lecterns were made for export in many Belgian workshops during the fifteenth and sixteenth centuries. Here, the boldly modeled eagle, symbolizing, perhaps, the Gospel of St. John, triumphs over evil in the form of the basilisk.

VIRGIN AND CHILD ON THE CRESCENT MOON. Polychromed and gilt poplar.
Lower Austria, ca. 1450-1460.   H. 70 in., w. 19¾ in., d. 8½ in. *Centennial
Purchase Fund. 65.1354*
Carved from a single piece of wood, and retaining most of its original
polychromy and gilding, the Austrian Virgin, presented as the apocalyptic
Virgin standing on the moon, is one of the finest extant examples of the Gothic
type of *Schoenen Madonnen.* The image of the wide-eyed gangling child,
however, far from the infant-ruler type of the earlier middle ages, gives the
group a compelling and intimate human quality that contrasts with the remote
beauty of the figure of the Virgin. Late Gothic realism characterizes the
expressive features of the moon and also the drapery, organized in deep angular
folds that underline the gentle sway of the Virgin as queen.

BAPTISMAL FONT. Goteke Klinghe of Bremen. Brass. Signed and dated 1483.
H. 3 ft. 7 in.   *Alice H. Goddard and Sarah F. Gorham Funds. 41.561*
The vessel, decorated with reliefs depicting the Crucifixion and the Apostles
under Gothic arches, and carried by four figures holding unidentified coats of
arms, demonstrates the technical perfection of this famous Lower Saxon family
in the casting of fonts and bells.

ST. CHRISTOPHER. Attributed to Brunellesco (1379-1446) and Nanni Di Banco (active 1405-1421). Bronze. Florence. Dated 1407. H. 8 in. *Arthur Tracy Cabot Fund. 51.412*

Unique in that it is one of the earliest examples of a Renaissance bronze statuette in the round, this figure is highly important in the evolution of Florentine art of the Quattrocento. Despite its small dimensions, the statuette has a compelling monumentality. The plasticity and quality of style make it obvious that the piece was created by an artist who had come under the strong influence of Ghiberti.

PORTRAIT BUST: Glazed polychromed terracotta (Hafner Ware). Salzburg, ca. 1500. H. 23 in. *Gift of R. Thornton Wilson in memory of the late John Fitzgerald Kennedy, thirty-fifth President of the United States. 64.1*

Northern late Gothic sculpture always stressed psychological expression. But it would be hard to find in this period a portrait bust that renders human dignity and suffering with more conviction. Coming from a wayside chapel near the Augustinian abbey of Gars on the river Inn in the Diocese of Salzburg, it is in likelihood a donor portrait — perhaps a self-portrait of the master of the renowned Salzburg Hafner Guild who made the bust.

MADONNA OF THE LILIES. Luca della Robbia, Italian (1399-1482). Glazed terra-cotta. Florence, ca. 1460-1470. H. 1 ft. 7 in., w. 1 ft. 3 in. *Gift of Quincy A. Shaw, through Quincy A. Shaw, Jr., and Mrs. Marian Shaw Haughton. 17.1476*
This composition is more elaborate than many of the "Rovezzano Madonna" types associated with Luca, by virtue of the inclusion of three angels hovering amidst blue and black clouds in the background, adoring the Mother and her Child. The finely modeled drapery and the delicately worked pale yellow flower in the foreground as well as the lilies themselves lend an especially graceful air to the composition. Unlike Donatello, Luca does not attempt to suggest unlimited expansion into space, but places the figures serenely in a well-defined shallow area. Although he was little interested in problems of perspective and anatomy that attracted so much attention in his day, his compositions convey a strong respect for nature and a deep religious reverence for his themes.

MADONNA OF THE CLOUDS. Donatello, Italian (1386-1466). Marble, in ex-tremely low relief. Florence, ca. 1425-1428. H. 13 in. *Gift of Quincy Adams Shaw through Quincy A. Shaw, Jr., and Mrs. Marian Shaw Haughton. 17.1470*
This early masterpiece by the great sculptor of the Florentine *quattrocento* is one of the very few accepted works by the artist in the United States. Donatello employs in the relief an original technique — very low relief and inscribed forms — called *rilievo schiacciato*. By means of this device, used first in his *St. George* relief at Or San Michele in Florence, the sculptor managed to create a believable illusion of space around the Madonna, who is surrounded by angel and putti in front and behind her. The "Shaw Madonna" will greet the visitor to Boston, as proof of Donatello's genius as an innovator, an extraordinary techni-cian, and sensitive interpreter of one of the favorite themes of Christian art.

MEDAL WITH SCENES FROM THE BOOK OF REVELATIONS. Signed Hans Reinhart the Elder (1538-1581), dated 1539. Silver. Germany.   Diam. 2⅝ in. *Theodora Wilbour Fund in memory of Zoë Wilbour. 68.50*
Designed by Hans Reinhart the Elder, an outstanding medalist of the German Renaissance, this medal dramatically presents scenes from the Book of Revelations that are inspired by prints of the period. Such medals were prized collectors as they are today.

BUST OF A LADY. Majolica. Tuscany (Florence or Caffagiolo), ca. 1500. H. 21 in *William F. Warden Fund. 54.146*
Apparently unique because of its size, this majolica bust is rare also because it takes the form of the human figure and, possibly, a portrait. The Florentine lad presents a very bright and lively image, well born, richly dressed in bright colo a jeweled necklace about her neck.

BUST OF CLEOPATRA. Pier Jacopo Alari Bonacolsi, called "Antico" (ca. 1460-1528). Bronze. Mantua.   H. 25⅜ in., w. 19¼ in. *William Francis Warden Fund. 64.2174*
The bronze bust of Cleopatra owes a heavy debt to the art of classical antiquity while it conveys a soft and dreamy quality of mood that is arresting. There are three busts in Vienna, *Ariadne, Bacchus,* and *Antinous,* which, with the Boston Cleopatra, may have been made for the small study of Isabella d'Este in Mantua.

BUST OF A PROPHET. Attributed to Sebastian Loscher, German (active 1510-1548). Lindenwood. Augsburg.   H. 24 in. *William F. Warden Fund. 49.4*
This is the only surviving example of a series of busts made for the stalls in the Fugger Chapel in Augsburg (1512-18) the decoration of which is the documented work of Adolph Daucher (1465-1523) and Sebastian Loscher. During the restoration of the chapel in 1832, the stalls were removed and the busts, with the exception of the one in Boston, were recut and overpainted and sold to the Berlin Museum in 1848. They were eventually destroyed during World War II. The bust demonstrates that extraordinary attention to detail and expressive power that characterize the best of northern Renaissance sculpture.

CHIMNEYPIECE: JUDITH WITH THE HEAD OF HOLOFERNES (detail). French, follower of Jean Goujon. Limestone. ca. 1560. H. 1 ft. 3 in., w. 1 ft. 6 in. *Gift of Mrs. Joseph Brummer and Ernest Brummer in memory of Joseph Brummer. 48.371*
The chimneypiece assumed importance as a work of monumental sculpture rather than decoration in late Renaissance Italy and France. This is one of the finest to survive from French art of the mid sixteenth century and comes from the Château de Bourg-Vexin, owned by the marquises de Bourg. The restraint and clarity of the figure, the elongated proportions, the incised outlines, all suggest that a sculptor of superior ability influenced by Jean Goujon produced this piece. Other portions of the composition depict Joshua in the war against Gideon slaying the five kings brought out of the cave.

ARCHITECTURE. Giovanni Bologna, Flemish (1525-1608). Bronze. Florence, ca. 1570. Signed GIO. BOLOGNE on lower edge of drawing board.   H. 14½ in. *Maria Antoinette Evans Fund and 1931 Purchase Fund. 40.23*
This small graceful figure is a fine example of the work of Giovanni Bologna, who, though originally Flemish, became a major force in Italian High Renaissance sculpture in Florence. The sculptor's inventions of allegorical and mythological figures were copied by his followers and other artists all over Europe through the seventeenth and eighteenth centuries. Architecture is a nude female figure in repose: she holds a board in her left hand and in her right the symbolic tools of an architect — a square, compass, and protractor.

STATUETTE OF HADRIAN. Gilt bronze, calcite crystal, calcite marble. Greco-Roman, 4th century and Italy, ca. 1550.   H. 22½ in. *Gift of the Class of the Museum of Fine Arts, Mrs. Charles Devens, Chairman. 1972.354*
The fascination of this object lies not only in its extraordinary beauty but also in the fact that it unites two different art historical periods. The torso and trunk of the figure is Late Antique and appears as a huge, reflective, semi-precious stone. The expressive, finely made gilt bronze head and hands were added in the Renaissance at the same time the base was repaired with matching stone. The statuette of Hadrian is the kind of object that might have found a place in a princely "art and curiosity" collection in the sixteenth century, while in its subject and form, the figure summarizes High Renaissance fascination with the world of antiquity.

DEATH TRIUMPHANT. Fruitwood. Lorraine (?), late 16th century.   H. 12¾ in.
Seth K. Sweetser Fund. 55.981
The subject, ultimately derived from the popular late Gothic "Dance of Death"
series, is intended as a moral allegory. The realistic rendering of tattered
scraps of skin and flesh curling off the bones and the dancing elegance of the
figure reflect the style and spirit of Callot and Ligier Richier.

STATUETTE OF MAX EMANUEL II OF BAVARIA. Giuseppe Volpini, German
(1662-1726). Marble. After 1714.   H. 20½ in. *William E. Nickerson Fund. 59.177*
The small marble statue exemplifies the idealized baroque ruler portrait. Pur-
poseful, hands on baton and sword, drapery behind, the figure looks upward
and beyond as if divinely inspired. Notable is the extraordinary detail with
which the sculptor to the Munich court has portrayed his illustrious patron.

MODEL FOR A PULPIT. Attributed to Joseph A. Feuchtmay (b. Austria, 1696,
d. Baden, 1769). Polychromed wood, partly gilded.   H. 33 in. *Seth K. Sweetser
Fund. 55.967*
The model for a pulpit represents a design for a project as yet unidentified,
which may in fact never have been executed. Such a model would have provided
either architect or patron with a clearer idea of the final result than any drawing.
Typical of the Central European rococo are the high drama and lively movement
that characterize figures, ornament, and architectural detail.

SLEEPING ENDYMION. Agostino Cornacchini, Italian (1685-1740). Terracotta. 1716.
H. 13¼ in. *H. E. Bolles Fund. 56.141*
The Sleeping Endymion is an extremely finely finished terracotta model upon
which were based bronze, marble, and porcelain versions of the subject. The
surviving related sculptures indicate that the composition originally included a
bank of clouds behind the figure that supported the crescent moon symbolizing
Diana drawn to the beauty of the sleeping Endymion.

ST. JOHN. Polychromed limewood. Austrian, ca. 1740. H. 6 in. *William F. Warden Fund. 1972.46*
By an artist as yet unidentified, this piece represents a most important example of Austrian Baroque sculpture of the eighteenth century. To understand the beauty and meaning of the subtle facial expression and the position of the figure as a whole, one must be aware that this statue was originally part of a group representing St. John supporting the Virgin fainting under the cross. A portion of the original paint has been lost from the face, allowing one to see even more clearly with what virtuosity and sensitivity the features were carved.

MADONNA OF VICTORY. Signed and dated 1771 by Johann Martin Mutschele, Bamberg (1733-1804). Schrezheim faience, white glazed. Contours and certain details purposely left unglazed. H. 48½ in. *William F. Warden Fund. 61.1185*
Made for the niche over the door of the Prinzen Inn of the Deutsche Orden at Wolframs-Eschenbach, this is a most important creation of German faience. The visionary concept and the dramatic movement of the drapery fully absorb the rococo style without forsaking the inherent local tradition.

ANDIRONS. Attributed to P. P. Thomire, French (1751-1843). Gilt and chased bronze. Paris ca. 1780. H. 1 ft. 8 in., w. 1 ft. 6 in. *Swan Collection, bequest of Miss Elizabeth Howard Bartol. 27.521*

A carefully ordered composition, essentially a pyramid on a rectangle, combined with more graceful, classicizing motifs of grapes, vines, cupids, goats, and a thyrsus mark these andirons as a fine example of Louis XVI ormolu. The bold forms of the goats and structure upon which they stand lend strength, and the finely cast and chiseled garlands of flowers, vines, and acanthus leaf scrolls add delicacy. The underlying organization and finish of all elements impose a firm unity on the whole, worthy of the finest artistic production of the late eighteenth century.

WALL PANELS. Claude-Nicolas Ledoux, French (1756-1806). Four carved oak panels, painted in watercolors and gilt on gesso. Paris, ca. 1770-1772. H. 11 ft. 7 in., w. 2 ft. 6 in. *Purchased from general funds. 79.326-9*

These boiseries, brought from a salon of the Hotel Montmorency, Paris, in the 1850's by Peter Parker for his daughter at Beacon House, depict classical figures in an elegantly elongated style recalling the sixteenth century French sculptor Jean Goujon. Trophies of arms, musical instruments, and shields with the interlaced initials MO for Montmorency form the major motifs of the series The set was perhaps designed to fit an octagonal room, but as the Hotel Montmorency was destroyed in 1840, documentation is incomplete. The extremely fine modeling, chasing, and gilding, as well as the imposing size and elegant composition, mark these panels as outstanding examples of the Louis XVI style.

BUST OF CARACALLA. Attributed to David Kam from the factory "De Paeuw" (The Peacock). Blue and white Delftware. Dutch, 1718. H. 20½ in. *Gift of Dr. Lloyd E. Hawes. 1973.103*
Delftware busts of such large size are extremely rare. This ambitious piece is important not only as an unusual and beautiful example of Delftware but also as a document of the continuing fascination with the antique (see statuette of Hadrian above). Originally thought to be Marcus Aurelius, the figure is now identified as Caracalla. The excellence of the modeling and coloring in addition to the fine condition of the bust make it a major addition to the museum's collection of European ceramics.

PLATE. Majolica. Siena (1518-1522). 10⅞ in. *Harriet Otis Cruft Fund. 55.931*
Decorated with a running band of coiled foliage painted in blue, called à *porcellana,* this plate is one of the few surviving examples of Sienese pottery attempting to produce a substitute for the then coveted "blue-and-white" porcelain of the early Ming dynasty of China.

OVAL DISH. Bernard Palissy, French (1510?-1590). Lead enameled earthenware. France, second half of the 16th century. L. 22 in., w. 17½ in. *Arthur Mason Knapp Fund and anonymous gift. 60.8*
Among Palissy's most celebrated works are his platters in the *style rustique* made up of casts from plants, animals, and insects, a popular practice in the sixteenth and seventeenth centuries. The objects on the platter, a snake, fish, frog, shells, and leaves, are glazed in imitation of their natural colors, while the earth is mottled in several shades, a process perfected by Palissy. Obviously far less spectacular in conception and size than the grotto he designed for the Tuilleries Garden in Paris around 1570, the platter exhibits the same virtuoso techniques so prevalent in Mannerist art of the time, playing on reality and artifice in man-made "nature."

CRUET FOR OIL AND VINEGAR. Florence, ca. 1575. H. 4½ in. *Gift of the Estate of Henry Williamson Haynes through Miss Sarah H. Blanchard. 12.717*
Painted in blue with fishes, a crab, a frog, and an insect (from a model-book in the manner of Ligozzi), this cruet is one of the early specimens of so-called Medici Porcelain, a kind of "soft-paste" majolica ware made for the Grand Duke Francesco I (1574-1587) in the pursuit of the secret of producing true Chinese porcelain.

SOUP TUREEN AND STAND. Porcelain. Meissen, Germany, ca. 1740-45. Marked with crossed swords in blue; "25" incised on tureen, "27" on platter. Tureen: h. 12¼ in. x 9 in. x 10½ in.; stand, 15½ in. x 11¹³⁄₁₆ in. *Bequest of Forsyth Wickes 65.2072*
This magnificent tureen is decorated with battle scenes of the Austro-Turkish wars taken from Augsburg prints. Vertical panels of gold scrollwork and shaded gilt trellis patterns frame the scenes; finely painted insects and flowers, derived from engravings by J. S. Weinman, are scattered on the lid, which terminates in a boar's head finial resting on richly curving scrolls. The delicate balance between austere form, lively painted battle scenes, and sumptuous gilt orna- ment mark this piece as an outstanding production of early German hard-paste porcelain.

CHINESE FAMILY. Porcelain. Raised anchor and raised red anchor marks. Chelsea factory, England, 1750-53. H. 9 in. *Gift of Richard C. Paine. 30.328*
This group is adapted from an engraving by Balechon and Aveline after "Les Delices de l'enfance," by Boucher, as is an earlier Meissen piece. The figure of the kneeling boy is modeled separately from the main group, both to prevent possible accidents in firing such a complex piece and to render the engraved composition more faithfully. The separate figure has the Chelsea raised red anchor mark and the main group has the plain raised anchor mark, but this does not necessarily imply that they were made at different times. The sculptural quality of the work suggests the style of the Tournai sculptor, Joseph Willems, who became modeler in Chelsea in 1750.

COVERED TUREEN IN THE FORM OF A HEN AND CHICKS WITH STAND OF MATTED FIELD FLOWERS. Soft-paste porcelain. Chelsea factory, England, ca. 1755. Red anchor mark. Tureen: h. 10 in., l. 15 in.; stand: w. 15¼ in., l. 19 in. *Gift of Mrs. Sigmund J. Katz. 1972.1081 and 1972.1082*
This superb tureen from the high period of English soft-paste porcelain manufacture perfectly embodies several characteristics of the Chelsea factory: highly imaginative form coupled with great refinement of technique both in modeling and painting. The animal and flower subjects are among the most felicitous and intricately worked pieces from this factory and employ mostly English subject matter rather than the equally popular forms taken from Oriental or Meissen models. Fortunately the stand, missing from a similar tureen in the Campbell Collection, has remained with our tureen.

PAIR OF VASES. Painted by Caton. Soft-paste porcelain. Sèvres, France, 1779. H. 28 in. *Gift of the heirs of Helen L. Jacques. 38.65. Bequest of Miss Elizabeth Howard. 27.534*
The vases were made for the palace at Versailles and were brought to Dorchester, Massachusetts, by Colonel James Swan, where they remained until his death abroad in 1830. Sold at auction and separated by the sale in 1868, they came to the museum through two different bequests. Their imposing size and opulent "royal blue" color, together with finely painted scenes depicting Belisarius unfettering Justinian and Belisarius leaving prison, mark them unmistakably as part of the royal furniture. The elegant and restrained urn forms combined with references in the cartels on the reverse sides to Roman legions, the pine-cone finial, seen in classical vase-painting in the form of a Maenad's thyrsos, all make them splendid examples of the Louis XVI period and among the finest pieces from the Sèvres manufactory.

EUROPEAN DECORATIVE ARTS & SCULPTURE | 223

LADY'S WRITING DESK. Pierre Macret, French (1729-1796). Veneered, red, gold, and black lacquer. Paris, ca. 1760. Ormolu mounts, stamped "Macret" twice. H. 32½ in., w. 32¾ in., d. 17 in. *Bequest of Forsyth Wickes, Forsyth Wickes Collection. 65.2506*
An important cabinetmaker to Louis XV, Pierre Macret created furniture indicative of the precious taste of courtly society in the mid and later eighteenth century France. The shape of this desk, with its elegantly tapering, cabriole legs and curved, bombé sides, is accentuated by the bands of black lacquer, which, in effect, outline the piece. Fascination with the Orient and Oriental decoration is evident on the surfaces, which are decorated with gold chinoiserie scenes on a brightly lacquered red background. The interior is of tulipwood, with six drawers above a sliding compartment and a gold-tooled leather writing surface.

BANCONE. Walnut, Italy, ca. 1550. L. 80½ in. *William F. Warden Fund. 62.7*
This magnificent *bancone*, probably made to be used as a money-exchange desk, like the famous one in the Loggia del Cambio at Perugia, comes from a room in a palace in Palermo, decorated with stucco ornaments by Montorsoli in the manner of the carving of this desk. Its architectural and ornamental forms as well as the powerful style of the mermaids are indeed sufficiently clos to Montorsoli's documented works in Sicily, especially his two marble fountains at Messina (1547-1557), to attribute the desk to the master.

LADY'S WRITING TABLE WITH FIRESCREEN. Satinwood, purpleheart inlays. English, Regency, 1800-1805. H. 34 in., w. 30 in. *Gift of Richard Milhender. 1974.423*
Brilliant satinwood relieved by rich brown purpleheart have been combined in a sophisticated fashion to produce this early Regency writing table. Although ultimately based on a Sheraton design, the table demonstrates the maker's originality in his departure from the known design. Sheraton described the basic concept of a writing table with firescreen: "The convenience of this table is that a lady when writing at it may both receive the benefit of the fire and have her face screened from the scorching heat."

CONSOLE TABLE. After a design by the architect Joseph Effner, German (1687-1745). Gilded oak. Munich, ca. 1740. H. 33¾ in. *Helen and Alice Colburn Fund. 57.658*
The design of this splendid, richly carved and decorated console table is attributed to Joseph Effner, who was architect to the Bavarian court. It bears the arms of Austria and a portrait of Electress Marie Amalie of Bavaria. The mate to this table is in Frankfurt and bears a likeness of her husband, Elector Karl Albert of Bavaria. The style of the table is typical of the elegant, lively German *Rokoko*, while it demonstrates eighteenth century German court taste under a strong French influence.

GIRANDOLE. Gilded pine. England, ca. 1765. H. 47½ in. *Gift of Eben Howard Gay. 34.1325*
One of a pair of rococo girandoles that follow plate 178 in Thomas Chippendale's *Gentleman and Cabinet-Maker's Director* of 1762 in their major details, though they have been enriched by the addition of the fantastic crowning birds.

CHARLES II TRAY. Silver. London, Maker IB, 1669. L. 27¾ in., w. 18⅝ in. *Theodora Wilbour Fund in memory of Charlotte Beebe Wilbour. 1971.640*
The large tray, one of the very few that survive, was made to serve no other purpose than to decorate and draw attention to itself upon the table or sideboard upon which it stood. Though made in London, the tray owes something of its style to Holland and Germany while the central scene of Nessus and Deianeira probably finds its source in a composition of Rubens or one of his followers.

PEDESTAL SALT. Silver gilt and rock crystal. London, 1577-1578. Bird in shield mark. H. 7¼ in. *Theodora Wilbour Fund in memory of Charlotte Beebe Wilbour. 51.1618*
Preciously composed of gilt silver and crystal, this object demonstrates how a now common staple — salt — was prized several hundred years ago. The salt is elaborately decorated with typical sixteenth century mannerist ornament, caryatids at the corners, and in the center Venus and Amorini, while a drole figure of a bagpiper stands as the finial and handle for the cover.

HOUR GLASS. Silver gilt. England, ca. 1525-50. W. 7 in. *Theodora Wilbour Fund in memory of Charlotte Beebe Wilbour. 57.533*
Elaborate cast and stamped ornament decorates this superb instrument whose quality of design and execution is equaled by the ingenuity applied to the question of its use. The glass can be conveniently turned and locked to either arm without detachment from the bracket.

RACING TROPHY. Silver, engraved. Made by William Williamson; engraved by Daniel Pomarede. Dublin, 1751.   Diam. 13⅞ in., h. 8½ in. *Theodora Wilbour Fund in memory of Charlotte Beebe Wilbour. 1973.482*
The beauty and importance of the punch bowl derive not only from its size and handsome shape but also from the superb engraving that explains the origin of the bowl. The horse race that is commemorated here halfway encircles the bowl, and the arms of the competitors embrace the following inscription: "A prospect of the great Match Run on the Curragh Sept 5th 1751 for 1000 guineas between Black and All Black belonging to the Honble Sr Ralph Gore and Bajazit the Property of the Rt Honble the Earl of March won wth ease by the former."

NAUTILUS BEAKER (detail). Nautilus shell with silver mounts. Holland (The Hague), 1659. H. 11 in. *William F. Warden Fund. 63.1256*
Made for Admiral Gansneb Tengnagel. On the inner shell in *ajouré* is his coat of arms; on the outer shell are found engraved figures from the Commedia dell' arte after prints by Jacques Callot. The silver stand bears the marks for Jean Duvignon, The Hague, 1700.

SALVER. Silver, engraved. London, 1685. Marked S. H.   Diam. 13½ in. *Theodora Wilbour Fund in memory of Charlotte Beebe Wilbour. 50.2725*
The salver illustrated is joined in the collection by a tankard, and both are decorated with fanciful designs called "chinoiserie" which evoked for seventeenth and eighteenth century patrons and artists the distant and mysterious East. In England this fashion reached a high point in the 1680's. Although the inspiration was the Orient, the result was peculiarly European in character.

CAKE BASKET. Paul de Lamerie, English (1688-1751). Silver. London, 1744. H. 11⅝ in. with handle up; l. 14⅛ in. *Bequest of Forsyth Wickes, Forsyth Wickes Collection. 65.2307*
When Louis XIV revoked the edict of Nantes, many Huguenot artists sought refuge in England, bringing with them the French style of the late seventeenth century. One such was Pierre Platel, whose pupil, Paul de Lamerie, fashioned this cake basket. Lamerie's style leads from simplicity to a wholehearted adherence to French rococo forms, seen here in the rich combination of floral motifs, cherub heads, caryatids, shells, and feet with masks and rococo ornament. The arms of the Duke of Montrose are enclosed in beribboned garlands. Lamerie's work unquestionably places him among the finest late eighteenth century silversmiths, from both the technical and the stylistic points of view.

TABLE. George and François Honoré Jacob, French. Malayan mottled amboina wood (the original marble top was of so-called rouge royale marbre de Tirlemont); chiseled and cast mercury-gilt bronze. Stamped with the crowned N, COMP (iègne) and JACOB FRÈRES/R (ne) MESLÉE. Paris, ca. 1803. H. 36¾ in., w. 53¼ in., depth 36¾ in. *Gift of Mr. and Mrs. William P. Allis. 1972.1034*
This table is part of the royal furniture from the Château de Compiègne made for Napoleon Bonaparte by the brothers Jacob, with bronzes from the atelier of Philippe Thomire. Classicizing motifs such as the caryatids, urn, and griffins, combined with simple, sober form, characterize much of the Empire style. A similar rectangular table, also supported by four caryatids and stamped JACOB, is in the Grand Trianon in Versailles.

PAIR OF CANDLESTICKS. Paul Storr, English (1771-1844). Silver gilt. Fully hallmarked and marked with the maker's initials. London, 1823. H. 9⅜ in. *Theodora Wilbour Fund in memory of Charlotte Beebe Wilbour. 66.436-7*
The candlesticks not only illustrate Storr's well-known technical perfection but also are remarkable for their unusually free adaptation and interpretation of classical form. The leonine feet and the serpent twined around the shaft of the candlestick may both be found in the standard repertory of silversmiths and goldsmiths as far back as the seventeenth century, but the dynamism with which Storr infuses his forms marks him as one of the most vital of artists working into the nineteenth century.

JEWEL BOX. Jean Baptiste Claude Odiot, French (1763-1849). Vermeil. Paris, ca. 1802. L. 9½ in., w. 7 in., depth 5⅛ in. *Gift of Miss Salome H. Snow. 76.346*
Odiot has enriched the spare surfaces of a severe rectangular form with rich yet rigorous decorations consisting of winged nymphs in classical robes carrying heavy garlands. Other classicizing motifs such as lyres, vases, and laurel wreaths occur on the sides and lid, combined with acanthus leaf and ivy leaf moldings. The sober opulence of the box itself is crowned by a putto reaching for a pomegranate, which forms an elaborate handle. This jewel box was presented by Napoleon to the Empress Josephine in 1805. Ordered from Odiot in Paris, it expresses the finest work and design of the Directoire period.

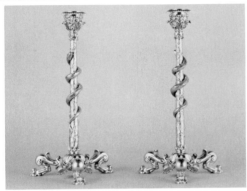

INKWELL. Sarah Bernhardt, French (1844-1923). Self-portrait as a Sphinx. Bronze, with plume added. Paris, ca. 1880. Engraved after casting on top of right base: "SARAH BERNHARDT: 1880." H. 12½ in., w. 7½ in. at base, d. 9 in. *Helen and Alice Colburn Fund. 1973.551*

In addition to a distinguished acting career, Sarah Bernhardt began to paint and sculpt around 1872 under the guidance of Georges Clairin and Gustave Doré. The epitome of the Art Nouveau woman, she here portrays herself as a beautiful, yet diabolical creature, exotic and mysterious. The sensitive modeling and imaginative symbolic composition of this inkwell reveal Bernhardt as accomplished in the fine arts as well as on the stage. The carefully chiseled finish and rich brown patination of the inkwell suggest the high levels of quality achieved by sculptors and founders in the nineteenth century.

VASE. Emile Gallé, French (1846-1904). Blown and engraved glass. Nancy, ca. 1905. Signature in cameo green overlay, "GALLÉ," preceded by a star. H. 13¼ in. *Gift of Arthur B. Nichols, in memory of his daughter Dorothy Nichols. 64.2002*

The sinuous lines of the raised floral decoration that wrap over the surface of this vase are typical of the École de Nancy, one of the foremost centers of Art Nouveau production in France. The artists in Nancy, even more than those in Paris, exaggerated the dynamic forms found in nature, creating a rhythmic linear style. Gallé worked in a wide variety of techniques, including free-blown, molded, inlaid, enameled, engraved, and etched glass, creating some of the most spectacular pieces of the nineteenth century. This vase is one of twelve in the collection that together show almost all aspects of his widely diversified styles.

CONSOLE TABLE. Michael Thonet, Austrian, ca. 1880. Rosewood top with ebonized bentwood legs. H. 29½ in., w. 43½ in., diam. 18¼ in. *Gift of J. Jonathan Joseph. 65.1192*

As early as 1860, the Thonet Brothers' factory in Moravia began experimenting with steam-bent wood; by the end of the century, their rocking chairs and tables were made for commercial as well as residential use. The graceful curves and loops of Thonet furniture, similar to the dynamic linear patterns seen in much Art Nouveau work, reflect a most happy marriage of design and technology. This console is one of three pieces of Czech bentwood in our collection, illustrating one of the earliest and most eloquent rejections of historicism in the nineteenth century.

EUROPEAN DECORATIVE ARTS & SCULPTURE | 235

SPRAY OF ASTERS. Peter Carl Fabergé, French (1846-1920). Rose gold, dyed blue agate, nephrite and rock crystal, no marks. Russia, St. Petersburg, 1896-1917. H. 6¾ in. *Bequest of Lila Stephenson. 1970.229*
One of five miniature vases with flowers in the collection, this bouquet illustrates Fabergé's delicacy and inventiveness: semiprecious as well as precious stones are often combined with several colors of gold or enameling to create objects of extraordinary luxury and refinement.

"SOYEZ AMOUREUSES VOUS SEREZ HEUREUSES." Paul Gauguin, French (1848-1903). Carved, polished, and polychromed lindenwood. Pont-Aven, Brittany, ca. 1889. With original frame. 47 x 38 in. *Arthur Tracy Cabot Fund. 57.582*
Carved after Gauguin's return from Martinique and anticipating his later Tahitian style, this relief combines images of passion and suffering with rich variations of surface texture, form, and applied color. In an 1889 letter to Emile Bonnard, Gauguin wrote that this relief is "the best and strangest thing I have ever done in sculpture . . . Gauguin (like a monster) taking the hand of a woman, who resists, and telling her: 'Be in love and you'll be happy.' " This carving joins two others in the museum's collections, and Gauguin's major painted work, *"D'où venons-nous, que sommes-nous, où allons-nous?"* in providing extraordinary insight into a complex and brilliant artistic personality.

LE PRINTEMPS. Jean-Baptiste Carpeaux, French (1826-1875). White marble. Paris, 1874. Signed and dated "J. Bte Carpeaux, 1874." H. 25 in. *Purchased through the Anna Mitchell Richards Fund. 37.1292*
This bust is taken from a plaster modeled by Carpeaux in 1870, now in the museum at Valenciennes. This version is essentially a variation on the head of Flora made by the sculptor for the Pavillon de Flore at the Louvre in 1866. Reflecting the often dry formulas favored by the Academy, Carpeaux sought to capture a moment instead of crystallizing the eternal. In the emphasis on shifting planes of form rather than on perfection of contours, *Le Printemps* as well as the sculpture executed by Carpeaux for the Paris Opéra radiate life and movement; narrative content is replaced by a preference for allegory or symbol without recourse to classicizing conventions. Our statue, formerly in the collection of M. Rainbeau (Napoleon III's natural son), is similar to another marble bust of the same title in the National Collection of Fine Arts, Washington.

HORSE GALLOPING ON RIGHT FOOT. Edgar Degas, French (1834-1917). Bronze, no. 47, cast L; stamped "Cire perdue. A. A. Hebrard"; between 1865 and 1881. H. 11⅞ in. Gift of Mrs. Margaret Sargent McKean. 1973.682

Degas was perhaps the most versatile and multifaceted artist of the latter nineteenth century, performing with equal facility as a painter, draftsman, printmaker and sculptor, constantly searching for the most expressive means of depicting form and motion. After Degas' death, an inventory of his studio revealed 150 works of sculpture, about 70 of which were salvageable for casting. This horse is one of a number of bronze figures shown at successive moments of stopped action, a favorite theme of Degas', often reworked as he strove to eliminate all possible excesses and strip figures down to their simplest, most true, unembellished form.

"LES PREMIÈRES FUNERAILLES." Auguste Rodin, French (1840-1917). Bronze, signed "A. Rodin" on surface of irregular mound; "Alexis Rudier, fondeur, Paris" at back bottom edge. Paris, ca. 1900.   H. 24 in., w. 20 in. Edwin L. Jack Fund. 59.52

Also called Le Purgatoire or La Tombée d'une âme dans les limbes, this group is one of Rodin's most accomplished and moving creations. It may well have been intended by Rodin that this piece be included in his most ambitious project, The Gates of Hell, commissioned in 1880 but never completed. In certain stylistic aspects, however, it is much more advanced and demonstrates an awareness of Degas' late sculpture.

THE GOLDEN FISH. Constantin Brancusi, Roumanian (1876-1957). 1924. Polished brass and steel. Signed and dated on underside edge of fish: "C. Brancusi — Paris, 1924." H. 5 ft., l. 1 ft. 4 in., d. 1 in., base diameter 1 ft. 8 in. *William F. Warden Fund. 57.739*

This work perfectly demonstrates Brancusi's dedication to the concept of pure, precisely streamlined form, enhanced by the play of light on the highly polished surfaces — here the abstract bronze fish and the mirrored steel base. The artist has attempted to convey the essence of the creature, "the flash of its spirit," as he said. Toward this end the fish is attached to its base by a pin, allowing it to float slowly, changing direction at the slightest touch. A rough wooden base carved by Brancusi for this piece was unfortunately lost before the sculpture came to the museum.

SEATED FIGURE AGAINST CURVED WALL. Henry Moore, English (1898-). 1956-1957. Bronze. L. 32 in. *Harriet Otis Cruft Fund. 59.477*

In this representative work of the fifties, Henry Moore shows his extraordinary sense for solid shape and volume and attacks once again a problem he has long been concerned with: the release of force, resulting from the interplay of mass and void in the human figure. He tries, in his own words, to "realize volume as the space that the shape displaces in the air," and to "relate and combine several forms, sections and directions into one organic whole."

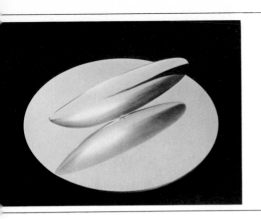

Musical Instruments Collection

TRANSVERSE FLUTE. Chevalier, Paris, ca. 1670-1680. Boxwood, ivory, and brass. 27¼ in. *17.1846*

Chevalier flourished within the circle of the Hotteterre family of musicians and musical instrument builders in the court of Louis XIV. The design of the "Hotteterre" flute was both revolutionary and significant. The new conical shape increased the range of notes that could be played, the addition of a key produced yet another note (E-flat) that could be used to correct the pitch of others, and the flute was made in three joints instead of one, which permitted adjustments in the overall pitch of the instrument. Its greater musical possibilities established its use in new instrumental ensembles at court, particularly in the orchestra. The elegantly undulating turnings reflect contemporary taste. Extant examples of the "Hotteterre" flutes are very rare. One of the earliest and finest is the museum's Chevalier, the only known example of his work.

BASS VIOLA DA GAMBA, division size. Arnif Rönnegrin (1680-1737). Lugede, Sweden, dated 1733. Spruce, maple, ebony, and bone. Total length 45⅛ in., body length 25¹³⁄₁₆ in., vibrating length of strings 25⅞ in.

Viola da gamba, or viol of the leg, is the generic name for the family of instruments in graduated sizes from treble to bass, with six strings tuned in intervals of a fourth and having a fretted neck. All sizes are held vertically cradled between the knees and played with a bow held underhand. This technique of bowing prevents the performer from exerting pressure on the strings and forcing the sound. The result is a delicate, responsive, reedy tonal quality, unlike that of the violin family. The division size of the viol is slightly smaller than the full bass and more suitable for playing the brilliant solo literature that was written for it between 1650 and 1800.

CLAVICHORD. Onesto Tosi, Genoa, Italy, 1568. Pine, boxwood, brass, and iron. Case dimensions, 11¾ in. x 46¾ in. *17.1796*

One of the earliest extant clavichords, the 1568 Onesto Tosi represents a standard Renaissance clavichord system. The clavichord, precursor of the piano, produces a sound when a tangent or thin piece of metal attached perpendicularly to the end of the key lever is struck against a string that is stretched from a hitch-pin on one end of the clavichord over a bridge to a tuning pin on the other end. The tangent acts as a temporary second bridge and serves two functions. When the tangent hits the string it determines the pitch by dividing the string, and it produces the sound by causing the string to vibrate. On the other side of the tangent, between the hitch-pin and the tangent, a ribbon of damper cloth is woven in between the strings, preventing the remaining portion of string from vibrating. The compass of the Tosi clavichord is C/E to c ′ ′ ′, or forty-five notes. It has only twenty-two pairs of strings, however.

DEPARTMENT OF PAINTINGS

Paintings have formed a major part of the collections of the museum since its founding in 1870. Yet it was only upon the appointment of a Keeper of Paintings in 1902 that the department emerged as a formal entity. Especially in earlier years, but even now, the character of the collection is formed by the tastes of Boston's collectors, whose generous gifts and bequests fill the galleries. Their influence has been exerted both through the donation of actual objects and through the gift of funds that make possible the purchase of otherwise unavailable works. In less than a century the painting collection has grown to become one of the world's foremost, ranging in date from the eleventh to the early twentieth century (contemporary art is discussed under that department heading).

Several segments are outstanding in regard both to quality of individual masterpieces and in depth of representation. For instance, French painting from the second quarter of the nineteenth century to approximately 1900 is equaled by no more than six other museums in the world. Boston collectors were among the first to appreciate the revolutionary developments of nineteenth century French art. Masterpieces by Delacroix, Courbet, Corot, Millet, and other Barbizon artists appeared in the United States first in Boston collections. Works by the Impressionists especially — Monet, Manet, Pissarro, Sisley, and Renoir — were eagerly sought by Bostonians and were ultimately donated to the museum. For example, of the thirty-four paintings by Monet in the collection, all but two were donated. Similarly, the masters of Post-Impressionism, Gauguin, van Gogh, Cézanne, and others, are all represented by major works, and in certain instances, such as the famous *D'où Venons-Nous? . . .* by Gauguin, by paintings of unrivaled importance.

Foremost among the many major donations to the French collection are the John T. Spaulding Bequest of nearly one hundred paintings and the

Quincy Adams Shaw Collection of nearly seventy paintings and pastels by Jean François Millet. Of great importance also are the works in the Juliana Cheney Edwards Collection and those given by Martin Brimmer, Denman Ross, Robert Treat Paine II, and Henry C. and Martha B. Angell.

Appropriately, the Boston collection of American art is one of the finest in the country. The homes of a city of historic and cultural tradition have provided their museum with a detailed panorama of painting in eighteenth and nineteenth century America. Particularly significant are the Colonial and early Federal portraits, dominated by over sixty works by John Singleton Copley and more than fifty by Gilbert Stuart, the great majority of which were given by the descendants of the sitters. Of similar importance is the M. and M. Karolik Collection of American Paintings from 1815 to 1865. The collection also contains an unusually large and fine group of paintings by the romantics and realists of the latter part of the century: Winslow Homer, Thomas Eakins, James McNeill Whistler, and Mary Cassatt.

Of the other European schools, the painting of Spain, Venice, and the Netherlands is well represented. Spanish works range from the extraordinary group of twelfth century Catalonian frescoes and an exceptional altarpiece by the fifteenth century Aragonese master, Martin de Soria, to a group of major works of the sixteenth and seventeenth centuries dominated by outstanding portraits by El Greco and Velásquez. The Venetian tradition is outlined from its early days through the late eighteenth century by a fine altarpiece by Bartolommeo Vivarini and numerous works by the sixteenth century masters, Titian, Tintoretto, Veronese, and Lotto, and by those of the eighteenth century artists, Guardi, Canaletto, and Tiepolo. Early Italian art is accented by the precious altarpiece of the Crucifixion by the Sienese master Duccio. Both Florence and Siena of the early Renaissance are represented by works of quality by Fra Angelico, Giovanni di Paolo, and Barna da Siena. An extremely rare work by the sixteenth century Mannerist innovator, Rosso, keynotes this important period.

The apex of the Netherlandish collection is the superb *Saint Luke Painting the Virgin,* by Rogier van der Weyden, given in 1893 by Mr. and Mrs. Henry Lee Higginson. Second only to it is an extraordinary anonymous Flemish triptych of the last quarter of the fifteenth century, representing the martyrdom of Saint Hippolytus. Another major work dated 1527 is the large and rare tempera painting by Lucas van Leyden, *Moses after Striking the Rock.* The leading masters of the seventeenth century, Rubens, van Dyck, Rembrandt, Frans Hals, and Ruisdael, are all represented by outstanding examples.

Works from the Baroque and Rococo movements in France and England, though not extensive, do include masterpieces by Poussin, Claude Lorrain, Bourdon, Boucher, and Chardin. In 1965 representation of the arts of eighteenth century France was significantly strengthened by the Forsyth Wickes Bequest, which included thirty-seven paintings, pastels, and minia-tures.

TIME UNVEILING TRUTH. Giovanni Battista Tiepolo, Venetian (1696-1770).   Oil on canvas, 91¼ x 66 in. *Charles Potter Kling Fund. 61.1200*
This magnificent allegory, called by the nineteenth century French critic Henri de Chennevières "the most beautiful painting from the easel of Tiepolo," is one of the monuments of all Venetian rococo art. Its splendor of conception, with the provocative and exotic symbols of base transience below the towering beauty of Truth, provided Tiepolo with an ideal vehicle for his virtuosity of brushwork and sumptuous color.

Reynolds, and Lawrence, several of which are from the collection of the late Governor Alvan T. Fuller.

A view of some of the major artistic movements of the twentieth century is also provided by the collection. American paintings of the earlier part of the century, especially the school of "The Eight," are shown in depth. Some of the major developments in Europe are outlined by works by the Cubists Picasso and Braque, and Gris and Feininger, and by the German Expressionists Kirchner, Beckman, and Kokoschka, and by younger men, Giacometti, Appel, Nicholson, and De Staël.

Mention should be made of the collection of miniatures by European and American artists such as Smart, Copley, and Malbone.

Publications concerning the collections include the *Summary Catalogue of European Paintings in Oil, Tempera and Pastel,* 1955; the catalogue of the *M. and M. Karolik Collection of American Paintings, 1815-1865,* published in 1949; the abridged catalogue of this collection with color illustrations; and the catalogue of *The Collections of John Taylor Spaulding, 1870-1948,* issued in 1948. A general discussion of the Forsyth Wickes Collection was published in 1968, and in the following year appeared an extensively illustrated, exhaustive catalogue of the American paintings in the museum.

FEMALE SAINT. Byzantine from Jerusalem, 11th century. Fresco.   15 x 11¼ in.
Maria T. B. Hopkins Fund. 51.1620
This fresco fragment and three others, torn from the walls of the Holy Cross
Abbey near Jerusalem, were discovered there in 1910 by Prince Johann Georg
of Saxony and purchased for his private collection. The original limelike fresco
plaster was mixed with straw and yarn, a method described in the *Painter's
Guide of Mount Athos* (A. N. Didron, *Manuel d'iconographie chrétienne*, 1845).

BYZANTINE FRESCO FROM THE APSE OF THE CHURCH OF SANTA MARIA DE
MUR. Catalonian, 12th century. Fresco. Approximately 22 x 24 ft. *Maria
Antoinette Evans Fund. 21.1285*
This large fresco, transferred in toto from the apse of the Romanesque chapel of
Santa Maria de Mur at a Benedictine Monastery in Catalonia, is undoubtedly the
best preserved and most important of Catalonian frescoes outside Spain. In
iconography and style its origins are Byzantine; the Apocalyptic Vision of Christ
in Majesty with symbols of the four Evangelists, and below the twelve Apostles
and scenes from the Nativity, are arranged in the Eastern hieratic manner. The
clear, vivid colors, reminiscent more of mosaic than fresco, suggest a parallel
relationship with the Byzantine mosaics at Monte Cassino, south of Rome.

CRUCIFIXION: ST. NICHOLAS AND ST. GREGORY (wings). Duccio di Buonin-
segna, Sienese (1255-1319). Tempera on panel.   24 x 31 in. overall. *Grant Walker
and Charles Potter Kling Funds. 45.880*
This triptych is the finest and best-preserved example in the United States of one
of Italy's greatest painters. Closely related in date and subject to his well-known
Maesta, the painting exemplifies his liberation of the human form from the
stiff and hieratic patterns of Byzantine art. He humanizes a traditional subject
with dramatic rhythms and the decorative beauty of color. Simone Martini, a
student of Duccio, has been suggested as the author of the wings, which are
surely by a separate hand.

VIRGIN AND CHILD. Barnaba da Modena, Modenese (active 1364-1383). Tempera
on panel. 39⅛ x 25 in. *Gift of Mrs. Walter Scott Fitz. 15.951*

THE MARRIAGE OF ST. CATHERINE. Barna da Siena, Sienese (ca. 1320-1356).
Tempera on panel.   53 x 42⅛ in. *Sarah Wyman Whitman Fund. 15.1145*

THE VIRGIN OF HUMILITY. Giovanni di Paolo, Sienese (1403-1482). Tempera on panel. 22 x 17 in. *Maria Antoinette Evans Fund. 30.772*

PORTRAIT OF A DOGE. Gentile Bellini, Venetian (1429-1507). Oil and tempera on panel. 21½ x 17 in. *Anna Mitchell Richards Fund. 36.934*

PRESENTATION OF THE VIRGIN IN THE TEMPLE. Master of the Barberini Panels, Italian, late 15th century. Oil and tempera on panel. 58 x 38½ in. Charles Potter *Kling Fund. 37.108*

This painting and its companion, the *Birth of the Virgin* (Metropolitan Museum), are presently attributed to the Master of the Barberini Panels because they were originally in the famous Barberini Collection, Rome. Their great beauty and eclectic style have provoked numerous attributions: to Fra Carnevale, a pupil of Piero della Francesca, and to the great painter-architects, Bramante and Alberti. Disregarding the question of authorship, in their graceful sense of light, air, and color, the panels mark a major moment in the Renaissance search for rationality and naturalism.

VIRGIN AND CHILD WITH ANGELS, SAINTS, AND DONOR, ca. 1445. Fra Angelico, Florentine (1387-1455). Tempera on panel, 11⅝ x 11½ in. *Gift of Mrs. Walter Scott Fitz. 14.416*
The kneeling donor to the left of the Virgin is one of the few portrait heads found in the work of Fra Angelico. The saints shown in the picture include St. Peter holding the keys, St. Paul behind him, and St. George on the right of the Virgin.

MADONNA AND CHILD WITH ST. JEROME AND ST. ANTHONY OF PADUA, ca 1521-1522. Lorenzo Lotto, Venetian (ca. 1480-after 1556). Oil on canvas, 37 x 30½ in. *Charles Potter Kling Fund. 60.154*
Before cleaning, this painting was considered a copy but has since been recognized as a work by Lotto. The composition is identical to a version in the National Gallery, London.

ST. CATHERINE OF ALEXANDRIA. Titian (Tiziano Vecellio), Venetian (ca. 1487-1576). Oil on canvas, 46⅜ x 39¼ in. *1948 Purchase Fund and Otis Norcross Fund 48.499*

THE DEAD CHRIST WITH ANGELS, ca. 1524-1527. Il Rosso Florentino, Florentine (1494-1540). Oil on panel. 52½ x 40¾ in. *Charles Potter Kling Fund. 58.527*
Considered "lost" until its recent discovery in a Spanish princely collection, this is the only complete work in America by the great leader of the Italian Mannerist movement and is probably the most important Mannerist painting in the United States. Clearly based on the art of Michelangelo and Leonardo, it radically contradicts Renaissance canons of harmonious balance and ordered space by means of vivid colors, abrupt lights and darks, and the tensions produced by the incongruities and distortions of massive forms in compressed space.

THE NATIVITY, ca. 1550. Tintoretto (Jacopo Robusti), Venetian (1518-1594). Oil on canvas, 61¼ x 143¼ in. *Gift of Quincy Adams Shaw. 46.1430*

SAINT SEBASTIAN, early 1630's. Bernardo Strozzi, Italian (1581-1644).   Oil on canvas. 65½ x 46 in. *Charles Henry Bayley Fund. 1972.83*
Saint Irene and her maidservant gently aid Saint Sebastian, wounded prior to hi
eventual martyrdom. This composition, presumably a preparatory work for
Strozzi's major altarpiece in San Benedetto in Venice, illustrates not only the
influence of Rubens but also that of Venetian artists on Strozzi, a Genoese, whe
spent his last thirteen years in Venice.

THE LUTE PLAYER, 1695-1700. Giuseppe Maria Crespi, Italian (1665-1747). Oil (canvas. 47¾ x 60¼ in. *Charles Potter Kling Fund. 69.958*
The Lute Player is more in the manner of his distinguished pupil, Piazetta, than Crespi's own, in which a predilection for portraiture and religious painting is apparent. An intimate genre scene of a musician tuning her instrument, the painting is vibrant with a senuous use of color and pigment.

BACINO DI SAN MARCO, VENICE, early 1730's. Antonio Canale (Canaletto), Venetian (1697-1768). Oil on canvas. 49⅛ x 80¼ in. *Abbott Lawrence Fund, Se K. Sweetser Fund, and Charles Edward French Fund. 39.290*
Apart from an English sojourn, Canaletto concentrated on depicting the topography of his native Venice. While his paintings provide an invaluable historical record, they transcend mere documentation and capture the essence of resplendent eighteenth century Venice, seen here from the terminus of the Grand Canal, the Palace of the Doge, the domes and campanile of S. Marco visible to the left, and the island and church of S. Giorgio Maggiore on the right.

RECEPTION OF A DIGNITARY, ca. 1763. Francesco Guardi, Venetian (1712-1793) Oil on canvas. 38¾ x 51¼ in. *Picture Fund. 11.1451*

RETABLE OF ST. PETER. Martin de Soria, Aragonese (active 1471-1487). Tempera on panel. 165½ x 220 in. overall. *Gift of Robert Hall McCormick. 46.856*

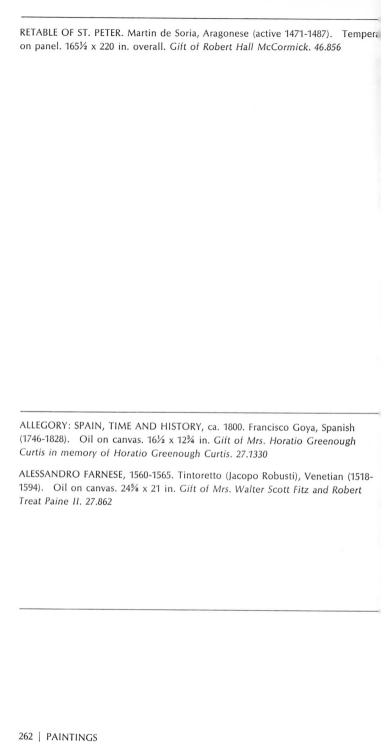

ALLEGORY: SPAIN, TIME AND HISTORY, ca. 1800. Francisco Goya, Spanish (1746-1828). Oil on canvas. 16½ x 12¾ in. *Gift of Mrs. Horatio Greenough Curtis in memory of Horatio Greenough Curtis. 27.1330*

ALESSANDRO FARNESE, 1560-1565. Tintoretto (Jacopo Robusti), Venetian (1518-1594). Oil on canvas. 24⅝ x 21 in. *Gift of Mrs. Walter Scott Fitz and Robert Treat Paine II. 27.862*

FRAY FELIX HORTENSIO PARAVICINO, ca. 1609. El Greco (Domencio Theoto-copuli), Spanish (1541-1614).   Oil on canvas. 44½ x 33¾ in. *Isaac Sweetser Fund. 04.234*
In the ruffled hair, ashen cheeks, brilliant eyes, and refined hands of Fray Felix, a Trinitarian poet and teacher, El Greco has powerfully interpreted an acute, nervous, and fiery personality. With deceptively modern simplicity and breadth of style he has created a dramatic and expressive painting that is generally considered his best portrait in an American collection.

DON BALTHASAR CARLOS AND HIS DWARF, 1631. Diego Velásquez, Spanish (1599-1660). Oil on canvas. 53½ x 41 in. *Henry Lillie Pierce Fund. 01.104*

The severe tension of Velásquez' early work, as in the museum's famous portrait of Luis de Gongora, relaxed under the warming influence of the great Venetian portraitists of the sixteenth century. His portrait of Don Balthasar Carlos, eldest son of Philip IV of Spain and Elizabeth of France, displays a new delight in free, full modeling of forms and the luxury of richly colored stuffs. His new technique and the subtle contrast with the dwarf emphasizes rather than undercuts the aristocratic bearing of the young prince.

DEATH OF THE VIRGIN. Bohemian, 14th century. Tempera on panel. 39 x 27¾ in. *William F. Warden Fund. 50.2716*

MAN OF SORROWS. Alsatian, 15th century. Oil on panel. 27¼ x 15¼ in. *Gift in memory of W. G. Russell Allen by his friends. 56.262*

THE LAMENTATION, ca. 1515. Lucas Cranach the Elder, German (1472-1554). Oil on panel. 15 x 10½ in. *Seth K. Sweetser Fund. 1970.348*

ST. LUKE PAINTING THE VIRGIN. Rogier van der Weyden, Flemish (1399/1400-1464). Oil on panel. 54¼ x 43¾ in. *Gift of Mr. and Mrs. Henry Lee Higginson. 93.153*
Although works by this distinguished master are numerous in America, this was the earliest major Flemish painting to enter an American public collection. Among the finest of Rogier's oeuvre, the painting was probably done for the Painters' Guild in Brussels and is now acknowledged as the original source for the three other versions held by major European museums. An early work of about 1436, it was directly influenced and inspired by Jan Van Eyck, but for his uncompromising realism is substituted the grace and elegance that mark the work of Rogier.

THE MARTYRDOM OF ST. HIPPOLYTUS (triptych), Flemish, last quarter of the 15th century.   Oil on panel. 39½ x 115 in. overall. *Purchased. 63.660*
This hitherto unknown and virtually flawless triptych depicting the brutal martyrdom of the third century Roman soldier Saint Hippolytus is one of the most extraordinary examples of early Flemish art in America. It has been suggested that the triptych's conception and completion are in fact the work of two artists whose participation was separated by an interval of time. Although the authorship is uncertain, an association with the school of Ghent and especially with the genius of Hugo van der Goes is evident in stylistic comparisons and in the skillful control of dynamic design and originality of composition. (Julius Held, *Album Disciplorum*, J. G. Van Gelder, 1973)

THE CRUCIFIXION. Joos van Cleve, Flemish (1485-1540/41).   Oil on panel. 31½ x 25 in. *Picture Fund. 12.170*

THE HEAD OF CYRUS BROUGHT TO QUEEN TOMYRIS, ca. 1623. Peter Paul Rubens, Flemish (1577-1640).   Oil on canvas. 80½ x 141 in. *Robert J. Edwards Fund. 41.40*
The genius of the great master of Northern Baroque art is revealed here in his bold but intricate design, vibrant color, and vivid visualization of the ancient tragedy from Herodotus. Rubens, with characteristic virtuosity, has blended the sweeping undulation of forms with brilliant textures, creating a composition of dramatic impact.

MOSES AFTER STRIKING THE ROCK, 1527. Lucas van Leyden, Dutch (1494-1533). Distemper on canvas. 72 x 90 in. *William K. Richardson Fund. 54.1432* Although best known as one of the finest masters of engraving of the Northern Renaissance, Lucas van Leyden was also a painter of high distinction, though few works remain. This painting, one of the three most important he produced (the others being in Leyden and the Hermitage, Leningrad), is a masterpiece of monumental design and superb draftsmanship. Its muted but sensitive coloring, the work of a man as at ease with the brush as with the burin, warms a scene of both classical drama and incidental anecdote.

WEDDING NIGHT OF TOBIAS AND SARA, 1611. Pieter Lastman, Dutch (1583-1633). Oil on panel. 16¼ x 22¾ in. *Juliana Cheney Edwards Collection. 62.985*

REV. JOHANNES ELISON and MEVR. JOHANNES ELISON (Maria Bockenolle), 1634. Rembrandt van Rijn, Dutch (1606-1669). Oil on canvas. 68⅛ and 68¾ x 48⅞ in. *William K. Richardson Fund. 56.510 and 56.511* These life-size full-length portraits, one of only two such pairs by Rembrandt, and in virtually flawless condition, synthesize the master's early style, his clarity of powerful expression. In these portraits, painted when he was only twenty-eight, Rembrandt has captured the robust presence of the English-born Dutch Reform pastor and his wife. Characteristically, space and form are revealed by Rembrandt's skillful handling of light. To this baroque factor he brings a penetrating observation of character that is typical of his portraiture.

A ROUGH SEA, ca. 1670. Jacob van Ruisdael, Dutch (1628/9-1682).   Oil on canvas. 42½ x 49⅛ in. *William F. Warden Fund. 57.4*
Probably the leading figure of the immense school of seventeenth century landscape in the Netherlands, this is among the most admired of Ruisdael's marines. More than any other, he infused his landscapes with stirring emotion made more powerful by his precise depiction of the awesome beauty of nature and man's frailty before the elements.

PORTRAIT OF A MAN, ca. 1664-1666, Frans Hals, Dutch (1580-1666).   Oil on canvas. 33½ x 26¼ in. *Gift of Mrs. Antonie Lilienfeld in memory of Dr. Leon Lilienfeld. 66.1054*

STILL LIFE WITH FRUIT. Isaak Soreau, German, born 1604.   Oil on panel. 24 x 35⅜ in. *Juliana Cheney Edwards Collection. 62.1129*

ANNE, LADY DE LA POLE, 1786. George Romney, British (1734-1802). Oil on canvas, 95½ x 59 in. *Given in memory of Governor Alvan T. Fuller by the Fuller Foundation. 61.392*
The highly refined and sophisticated flattery of eighteenth century British portraiture, derived from the art of van Dyck and ultimately the Venetian sixteenth century, is epitomized by this painting. Its graceful attenuation, skillful surfaces, and atmosphere of sweet but aristocratic gentility mark the painting as perhaps the best of Romney's portraits in America.

CAPTAIN THOMAS MATTHEW, 1772. Thomas Gainsborough, British (1727-1788). Oil on canvas. 29¾ x 24½ in. *Juliana Cheney Edwards Collection. 25.134*
Mention is made in a contemporary diary that the two portraits of Captain Matthew and his wife were seen in Gainsborough's studio in Bath in 1772. His delicate brushwork and refined sense of color and draughtsmanship enhanced the dignity and elegance of his confident sitters, and in this portrait the sketchiness of the costume adds an attractive sense of immediacy to an otherwise conventional portrait form.

THE SLAVE SHIP, 1840. Joseph Mallord William Turner, British (1775-1851). Oil on canvas. 35¾ x 48 in. *Henry Lillie Pierce Fund. 99.22*
Turner's use of color and light to define form increased progressively until his landscapes became highly atmospheric and nearly abstract. In this significant late work the subject, based in part on an actual incident and on passages from an eighteenth century poem by James Thomson, seems less important than the powerful swirling moment in which the drama takes place; the painting is principally a depiction of nature.

JEAN JACQUES CAFFIERI, 1784. Adolphe Ulrik Wertmüller, Swedish (1751-1811). Oil on canvas. 50¾ x 37¾ in. *Ernest W. Longfellow Fund. 63.1082*

THE STOUR VALLEY AND DEDHAM CHURCH, 1814. John Constable, British (1776-1837). Oil on canvas. 21¾ x 30¾ in. *William W. Warren Fund. 48.266*
Constable exerted a considerable innovative force in the formation of an English landscape tradition in the nineteenth century. Numerous drawings and sketches exist connected with this painting, indicating Constable's method of making preliminary on-the-site studies that were incorporated into the finished painting. It is documented as having been painted in 1814 as a wedding present from Thomas Fitzhugh to his bride, whose father then owned the field from which the view was taken.

PARNASSUS, 1680 (?). Claude Lorrain, French (1600-1682).   Oil on canvas.
38½ x 53 in. *Picture Fund. 12.1050*

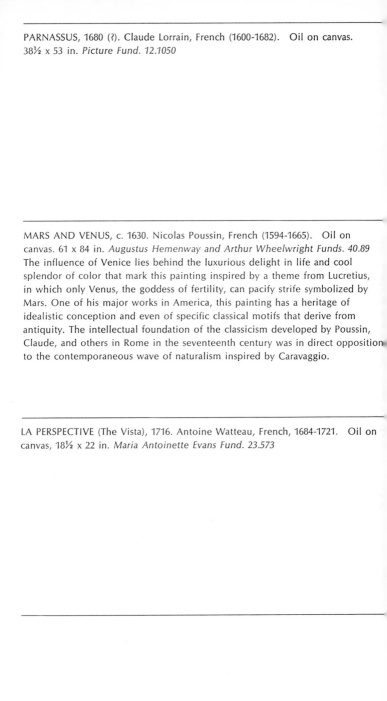

MARS AND VENUS, c. 1630. Nicolas Poussin, French (1594-1665).   Oil on
canvas. 61 x 84 in. *Augustus Hemenway and Arthur Wheelwright Funds. 40.89*
The influence of Venice lies behind the luxurious delight in life and cool
splendor of color that mark this painting inspired by a theme from Lucretius,
in which only Venus, the goddess of fertility, can pacify strife symbolized by
Mars. One of his major works in America, this painting has a heritage of
idealistic conception and even of specific classical motifs that derive from
antiquity. The intellectual foundation of the classicism developed by Poussin,
Claude, and others in Rome in the seventeenth century was in direct opposition
to the contemporaneous wave of naturalism inspired by Caravaggio.

LA PERSPECTIVE (The Vista), 1716. Antoine Watteau, French, 1684-1721.   Oil on
canvas, 18½ x 22 in. *Maria Antoinette Evans Fund. 23.573*

LE DÉJEUNER DE JAMBON (The Ham Luncheon), c. 1735. Nicolas Lancret, French (1690-1745). Oil on canvas. 27¾ x 18 in. *Bequest of Forsyth Wickes; Forsyth Wickes Collection. 65.2649*

With the Forsyth Wickes Bequest came this remarkably exuberant study for one of the decorations painted in 1735 by order of Louis XV for the dining room of the *petits appartements* at Versailles. Today the larger version and a pendant, *Le Déjeuner d'huitres*, by Jean-François de Troy (1679-1725), are in the Musée Condé in Chantilly. Lancret, like his contemporary Watteau, is best known for gallant scenes imbued with the elegance and fragile gaiety of the eighteenth century.

HALT AT THE SPRING, 1765. François Boucher, French (1703-1770). Oil on canvas. 82½ x 108¼ in. *Gift of the Heirs of Peter Parker. 71.2*

THE TEA POT, 1764. Jean Baptiste Simeon Chardin, French (1699-1779). Oil on canvas. 12¾ x 15¾ in. *Gift of Martin Brimmer. 83.177*

THE SOWER, 1850. Jean François Millet, French (1814-1875). Oil on canvas. 39¾ x 32½ in. *Gift of Quincy Adams Shaw, through Quincy A. Shaw, Jr., and Marian Shaw Haughton. 17.1485*
Millet's intention to ennoble the simple peasant was misunderstood by most of his contemporaries, who would have been able to view another version of *The Sower* at the Salon of 1850. The monumental figure outlined against the hill, his face in shadow, cannot be viewed as an individual but rather as representative of all humble laborers. Millet's disregard for traditional academic subject matter and his concentration on nature is typical of the Barbizon School of painters, of which he was a principal figure, but the sympathy expressed in his art for the peasant is uniquely his own.

OPHELIA, 1868-1870. Jean Baptiste Camille Corot, French (1796-1875). Oil on canvas. 27¾ x 18¼ in. *Bequest of David P. Kimball in memory of his wife, Clara Bertram Kimball. 23.511*

YOUNG SHEPHERDESS, 1869-1871. Jean François Millet, French (1814-1875). Oil on canvas. 64 x 44¼ in. *Gift of Samuel Dennis Warren. 77.249*

THE ENTOMBMENT, 1848. Eugène Delacroix, French (1798-1863). Oil on canvas. 63½ x 51¼ in. *Gift by contribution in memory of Martin Brimmer. 96.21*
Delacroix kept extensive, thoughtful journals throughout his life, and during 1847 he carefully recorded his progress on the *Entombment (Le Christ au Tombeau)*, his major painting of that year, finished in 1848. As he worked on the picture, he became worried about the difficulty of preserving the power of his original sketch, and he endeavored to keep the details and the background as simple as possible, to concentrate the effect of the picture in the foreground figures. We do not know how Delacroix felt about the painting at the time he finished it, since his 1848 diary has been lost (if ever it existed); but some years later he chose the *Entombment* for inclusion in the special exhibition of his works at the Universal Exposition of 1855, and he wrote that the sight of it had filled him with an emotion so strong that it surprised him.

ISLAND OF SAN BARTOLOMMEO, ROME, ca. 1827. Jean Baptiste Camille Corot, French (1796-1875).   Oil on canvas. 10½ x 17 in. *Harriet Otis Cruft Fund. 23.118*
While on his first trip to Italy in 1825-28, Corot made numerous studies *en plein air* exploring the qualities of light. This view of the well-known island in the Tiber in full Italian sunlight with strongly cast shadows in comparatively rich color has a clarity and concreteness that is not seen in Corot's later more lyrical, atmospheric work.

THE QUARRY, late 1850's. Gustav Courbet, French (1819-1877).   Oil on canvas. 83 x 71 in. *Henry Lillie Pierce Fund. 18.620*
This painting was brought to Boston by an art dealer in 1866, only a few years after it was painted in the late 1850's, making it one of the first French Realist paintings to enter the United States. Several young Boston artists were quite taken with the work, particularly Courbet's bold manner of painting with broad, heavy brush or palette-knife strokes, and in a matter of days they raised the substantial sum of $5,000 for its purchase by their art club.

Several visible seams in the painting suggest that Courbet composed the picture in a number of steps, probably beginning with a small picture of the roebuck, then sewing on new pieces of canvas as he decided to add the dogs and figures, as well as further landscape sections. The standing figure may be based on a photograph of the artist leaning against a tree.

EXECUTION OF THE EMPEROR MAXIMILIAN, 1867. Edouard Manet, French (1832-1883). Oil on canvas. 76¾ x 102 in. *Gift of Mr. and Mrs. Frank Gair Macomber. 30.444*

The depiction of the instant of execution of the Emperor Maximilian of Mexico in 1867, following French troop withdrawal, is reminiscent of Goya's painting of 1808, *Executions of the Third of May*. The immediacy of Manet's composition is heightened by the fact that he did not finish this first version. Others exist in the Ny Carlsberg Glyptotek, Copenhagen, and the Städtische Kunsthalle, Mannheim, and there are fragments in the National Gallery in London as well.

THE STREET SINGER, ca. 1862. Edouard Manet, French (1832-1883). Oil on canvas. 69 x 42¾ in. *Bequest of Sarah Choate Sears in memory of her husband, Joshua Montgomery Sears. 57.38*

The isolation of the figure and its placement against a dark tonal background illustrate the influence of Velásquez on Manet's early work. Victorine Meurend, a model frequently used at this stage of Manet's career, is shown appearing from the doorway of a café. The recreation of a casual incident, which the artist himself witnessed, for use as subject matter for a painting is one aspect of the Impressionists' break with orthodox academic ideals.

THE MUSIC LESSON, 1870. Edouard Manet, French (1832-1883). Oil on canvas, 55 x 67¾ in. *Given in memory of Charles Deering. 69.1123*

Despite its acceptance by the official Salon of 1870, *The Music Lesson* was not publicly well received, was in fact ridiculed, and the painting remained in the artist's studio. In 1884, however, it was selected to be shown in the memorial exhibition honoring Manet the year following his death. Interestingly, Manet posed Zacharie Astruc, a writer who supported the work of Manet and his friends, as the guitarist; his companion has not yet been identified.

FLOWERS AND FRUIT. Henri Fantin-Latour, French (1836-1904). Oil on canvas. 23½ x 28¾ in. *Bequest of John T. Spaulding. 48.540*

DUKE AND DUCHESS OF MORBILLI, 1867. Edgar Degas, French (1834-1917). O
on canvas. 45¾ x 35¼ in. *Gift of Robert Treat Paine II. 31.33*
This penetrating double portrait of the artist's sister, Thérèse de Gas, and her
husband remained in Degas' studio during his lifetime, withheld from public
view or sale, as were other family portraits. An early work, the painting display
both the influence of Ingres and Degas' own sensitive draftsmanship and
compositional skill to a marked extent.

DEUX JEUNES FEMMES VISITANT UN MUSÉE (Two young ladies visiting a
museum), ca. 1877-1880. Edgar Degas, French (1834-1917).   Oil on canvas. 35½ x
26 in. *Anonymous gift. 69.49*
Deux jeunes femmes visitant un musée belongs to a group of oils, pastels, and
prints made by Degas from 1877 to 1880, of a woman, sometimes with a
companion, in a museum. It has been suggested that the standing woman is
Mary Cassatt, because of her resemblance to a figure shown in a Degas pastel
of 1880 identified as Mary Cassatt in the Louvre.

CARRIAGE AT THE RACES, ca. 1872. Edgar Degas, French (1834-1917).   Oil on canvas. 13¾ x 21½ in. *Arthur Gordon Tompkins Residuary Fund. 26.790*
This small oil was included in the first Impressionist exhibition in Paris in 1874 and shows Paul Valpinçon, a friend of Degas' whom he depicted in other works, and his family in a carriage. Despite the actual size of the painting, through his unusual composition and suggestion of atmosphere, Degas has created a work of remarkable spaciousness.

LE BAL À BOUGIVAL, 1883. Pierre Auguste Renoir, French (1841-1919).   Oil on canvas. 70½ x 37¾ in. *Anna Mitchell Richards Fund and Contributions. 37.375*
Considered a masterpiece of Impressionist art, this painting shows the vitality and simple, unforced pleasure in feminine beauty and the joy of life that are the essence of Renoir's work. The slightly swaying life-size figures, dappled with summer sun, summarize the Impressionists' devotion to the conception of all life and nature as valid for art. In technique and approach, it is a synthesis of Impressionism.

LA JAPONAISE, 1876. Claude Monet, French (1840-1926). Oil on canvas. 91 x 56 in. *1951 Purchase Fund. 56.147*

The virtuosity of La Japonaise lies in its scale, execution, and departure from Monet's usual concentration on landscape or figures in a landscape setting. Monet described the painting in a letter of 1919 to Durand-Ruel: "It is not a painting of a Japanese, but better still, a French girl in a Japanese costume — it was my first wife who posed for me." The model is clearly French; however, the Japanese fans and the placement of the kimono-clad figure in a manner recalling Japanese Ukiyo-é paintings and prints clearly indicate Monet's receptiveness to aspects of Japanese art that exerted an influence on all of the Impressionists.

NYMPHÉAS; PAYSAGE D'EAU (Waterlilies), 1905. Claude Monet, French (1840-1926). Oil on canvas. 35¼ x 39¼ in. *Gift of Edward Jackson Holmes. 39.804*

ROUEN CATHEDRAL: SUNSET, 1894. Claude Monet, French (1840-1926). Oil on canvas. 39½ x 25¾ in. *Juliana Cheney Edwards Collection. 39.671*

HAYSTACK IN WINTER, 1891. Claude Monet, French (1840-1926). Oil on canvas 36¼ x 26 in. *Gift of Misses Aimée and Rosamond Lamb in memory of Mr. and Mrs. Horatio A. Lamb. 1970.253*

Monet, fascinated by light and its effect on color and form, repeatedly explored a commonplace motif as it changed with varying atmospheric conditions and at different times of day. His impressions, for example, of a haystack under winter snow, the façade of Rouen cathedral brilliant with borrowed color from a sunset, or waterlilies on a pond in his garden at Giverny, are single paintings in series devoted to these three individual subjects. They are among the several series painted by Monet during his lifetime.

D'OÙ VENONS-NOUS? — QUE SOMMES-NOUS? — OÙ ALLONS-NOUS? (Where do we come from? Who are we? Where are we going?), 1897. Paul Gauguin, French (1848-1903). Oil on canvas. 54¾ x 147½ in. *Arthur Gordon Tompkins Residuary Fund. 36.270*

This monumental and enigmatic painting that Gauguin executed directly on the canvas was done in Tahiti in one month in 1897 as a last testament before his suicide attempt, and was regarded by him, and now by later generations, as his masterpiece. Symbolically, it expresses the artist's conception of the course and quandary of human life. Artistically, it represents Gauguin's work at a moment when his fully developed powers, both of design and of symbolic color, were fused in the creation of a work of profound mood and significance.

MADAME CÉZANNE IN A RED ARMCHAIR, ca. 1877. Paul Cézanne, French (1839-1906). Oil on canvas. 28½ x 22 in. *Bequest of Robert Treat Paine II. 44.776* This portrait is dated by the wallpaper, which was in Cézanne's home in Paris at 67 rue de l'Ouest, where he lived in 1877. Cézanne is known to have painted at least twenty-six portraits of Marie-Hortense Fiquet, who became his wife in 1886.

SELF-PORTRAIT WITH A BERET, ca. 1898-1899. Paul Cézanne, French (1839-1906). Oil on canvas. 25 x 20 in. *Charles H. Bayley Fund and partial gift of Elizabeth Paine Metcalf. 1972.950*

Painted at the age of sixty, this was probably Cézanne's last self-portrait. His portrait of Madame Cézanne and this self-portrait, both originally in the collection of Egisto Fabbri, an artist who owned many of Cézanne's paintings, came to the museum through the collection of Robert Treat Paine II.

THE POSTMAN ROULIN, 1888. Vincent van Gogh, Dutch (1853-1890). Oil on canvas. 32 x 25½ in. *Gift of Robert Treat Paine II. 35.1982*
Van Gogh painted six portraits of the postman, a close friend of his in Arles. He did portraits of the entire Roulin family, including Madame Roulin, *La Berceuse,* which is in the collection as well.

"À LA MIE," 1891. Henri de Toulouse-Lautrec, French (1864-1901). Watercolor and gouache on millboard. 21 x 26¾ in. *S. A. Denio Fund and General Income for 1940. 40.748*
Parisian life toward the turn of the century in all its aspects served as inspiration for Toulouse-Lautrec, who objectively made notes of what he saw and painted without social comment, Toulouse-Lautrec's admiration of Degas is evident from the choice of subject matter, the directness, and the use of line to characterize form in this scene at the café La Mie. The composition in this instance was derived from a photograph taken on the artist's direction by a friend, the photographer Paul Sescau.

STILL LIFE WITH BLUE PLUMS, 1925. Georges Braque, French (1882-1963). Oil on canvas. 9 x 29 in. *Gift of Mr. and Mrs. Paul Rosenberg. 57.523*

RECLINING NUDE, 1909. Ernst Ludwig Kirchner, German (1880-1938). Oil on canvas. 29¼ x 59½ in. *Arthur Gordon Tompkins Residuary Fund. 57.2*

STANDING FIGURE, 1908. Pablo Picasso, Spanish (1881-1973). Oil on canvas. 59 x 39½ in. *Juliana Cheney Edwards Collection. 58.976*
This giant of twentieth century art is here represented by a work executed at a crucial point after the blue and rose periods and just prior to his Cubist experiments. Under the stimulus of primitive art, Picasso here embarked upon his analysis of the nature of forms that would ultimately determine the course of a major segment of the art of our time.

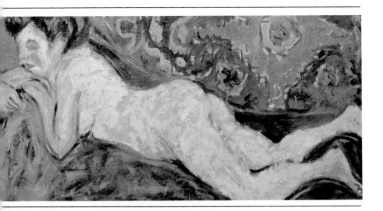

THE SABINES, 1963. Pablo Picasso, Spanish (1881-1973).   Oil on canvas. 77 x 51¼ in. *Robert J. Edwards Fund, Fanny P. Mason Fund, and Arthur Gordon Tompkins Residuary Fund. 64.709*
In contrast to *Standing Figure,* this work painted fifty-five years later is a vehement personal statement derived from a nineteenth century neo-classical painting by Jacques Louis David, *Les Sabines,* here used as a declamation against war. Violence is conveyed through the almost grotesque abstraction of form, the harshness of the color combined with heavy outlining, and the absence of space that causes the four figures seemingly to impinge upon each other. The painting is a synthesis of many developments and motifs in Picasso's work.

DOUBLE PORTRAIT OF TRUDL, 1931. Oskar Kokoschka, Austrian (born 1886). Oil on canvas. 39¾ x 28 in. *Seth K. Sweetser Residuary Fund. 61.1138*

THE VOICE, 1893. Edvard Munch, Norwegian (1863-1944).   Oil on canvas. 34½ x 42½ in. *Ernest Wadsworth Longfellow Fund. 59.301*
The Voice incorporates motifs repeated by Munch in other compositions around the turn of the century — a constrained frontal female figure, rigid pines, a reflection spreading out on the water — which emphasize a sense of isolation and anxiety. Munch's concern with psychological meaning and his expressive use of form and color greatly influenced artists of his own generation, notably the German Expressionists.

RUE GAUGUET, 1949. Nicolas de Staël, French (1914-1955). Oil on panel. 78½ x 94¾ in. *Arthur Gordon Tompkins Residuary Fund. 57.385*
Despite the brevity of his career, de Staël was perhaps the leading painter of his generation in France. In this work, based on a "memory picture" of Paris, he has created a monumental and dynamic design of highly sensitive color harmonies. Even his technique of employing thick planes of pigment, applied with hoe-like tools of his own design, emphasizes his statement.

American

PAUL REVERE, ca. 1768-1770. John Singleton Copley, American (1738-1815).
Oil on canvas. 34⅞ x 28½ in. *Gift of Joseph W., William B., and Edward H. R.*
Revere. 30.781
The informality of the pose in this portrait was highly unusual for Copley,
whose commissions from the wealthy Boston merchants ordinarily called for a
more elegant portrait. This is one of the few paintings showing a colonial
craftsman at work.

JUDGE SAMUEL SEWALL, 1729. John Smibert, American (1688-1751). Oil on
canvas. 30¼ x 25¼ in. *Bequest of William L. Barnard by exchange and Emily L.*
Ainsley Fund. 58.358
In 1692 Judge Samuel Sewall was appointed one of the special judges to try the
witches of Salem, Massachusetts.

ROBERT GIBBS, 1670. Freake Limner, American. Oil on canvas. 40 x 33 in.
M. & M. Karolik Fund. 69.1227
The attribution to the Freake Limner was established through this painting's
clear relationship to the portraits of John Freake and Mrs. Freake and Baby Mary
in the collection of the Worcester Museum, Worcester, Massachusetts, and is
the only seventeenth century American painting in the collection.

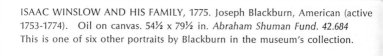

ISAAC WINSLOW AND HIS FAMILY, 1775. Joseph Blackburn, American (active 1753-1774). Oil on canvas. 54½ x 79½ in. *Abraham Shuman Fund. 42.684*
This is one of six other portraits by Blackburn in the museum's collection.

MARY AND ELIZABETH ROYALL, 1758. John Singleton Copley, American (1738-1815). Oil on canvas. 57½ x 48 in. *Julia Knight Fox Fund. 25.49*
This self-taught native genius, unquestionably the foremost figure of American art before the nineteenth century, in virtual isolation from the artistic currents of his day, developed his talents to surpass any of his contemporaries on this continent. Perceptive of observed nature he portrayed prosperous merchants, their ladies, and their families with an uncompromising and truthful eye, but one that obviously delighted in rich fabrics and colors.

WATSON AND THE SHARK, 1788. John Singleton Copley. American (1738-1815). Oil on canvas. 72 x 90⅛ in. *Gift of Mrs. George von Lengerke Meyer. 89.481*
This picture is a replica after the original painting, now in the National Gallery, Washington, D.C. Both pictures were done by Copley in 1778.

GEORGE AND MARTHA WASHINGTON, 1796. Gilbert Stuart, American (1755-1828). Oil on canvas. 39⅝ x 34½ in. *On deposit from the Boston Athenaeum. Ath. 1 & 2.*
Probably the best known paintings in American art, these portraits were done from life by Stuart in Philadelphia in 1796. Called the "Athenaeum Heads," the paintings have been owned by the Boston Athenaeum since 1831, shortly after the artist's death. The likeness of the first President served as a prototype for dozens of replicas by Stuart.

PASSAGE OF THE DELAWARE, 1819. Thomas Sully, American (1783-1872). Oil on canvas. 146¼ x 207½ in. *Gift of the owners of the old Boston Museum. 03.1079*
Commissioned for the Capitol Building of the State of North Carolina, this painting was too large for the space and was therefore rejected.

THE TORN HAT, 1820. Thomas Sully, American (1783-1872). Oil on panel. 19 x 14½ in. *Gift of Belle Greene and Henry Copley Greene, in memory of their mother, Mary Abby Greene. 16.104*
The young boy in the painting is the artist's son, Thomas Wilcocks Sully, who later became a portrait painter in Philadelphia.

ELIJAH IN THE DESERT, 1818. Washington Allston, American (1779-1843). Oil on canvas. 49 x 72½ in. *Gift of Mrs. Samuel Hooper and Miss Alice Hooper. 70.1*
The first registered acquisition of the museum in 1870. The subject was taken from the Bible, Kings, 1, 17: Elijah at the word of the Lord "went and dwelt by the brook Charith, that is before Jordan, And the ravens brought him bread and flesh in the evening."

JOSEPH MOORE AND HIS FAMILY, 1839. Erastus Salisbury Field, American (1805-1900). Oil on canvas. 82¾ x 93¼ in. *M. and M. Karolik Collection. 58.25*

REV. JOHN ATWOOD AND HIS FAMILY, 1845. Henry F. Darby, American (1829-1897). Oil on canvas. 72 x 96⅜ in. *M. and M. Karolik Collection. 62.269*
A self-taught portrait painter, Darby did this picture of the Atwood family when he was sixteen. The Darby family diary is preserved in the museum.

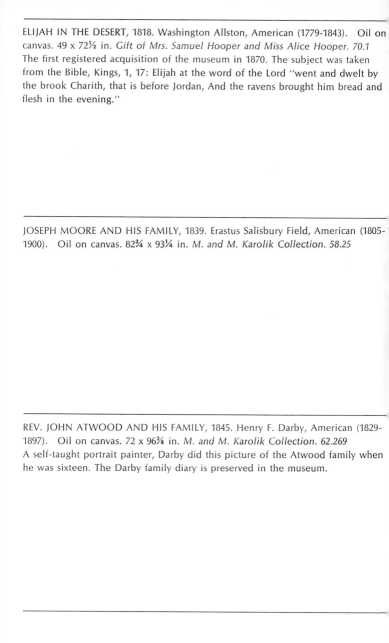

APPROACHING STORM: BEACH NEAR NEWPORT, 1860's. Martin Johnson Heade American (1819-1904). Oil on canvas. 28 x 58¼ in. *M. and M. Karolik Collection 45.889*
Possibly depicting Narragansett Bay, this is one of Heade's most dramatic paintings.

THE FOG WARNING, 1885. Winslow Homer, American (1836-1910). Oil on canvas. 30 x 48 in. *Otis Norcross Fund. 94.72*
Painted at Prout's Neck, Maine, where Homer lived after 1883, this picture was first titled *Halibut Fishing.*

LONG BRANCH, NEW JERSEY, 1869. Winslow Homer, American, 1836-1910. Oil on canvas. 16 x 21¾ in. *Charles Henry Hayden Fund. 41.631*
One of Homer's best known early pictures, done when he was living in New York.

THE LAGOON, VENICE: NOCTURNE IN BLUE AND SILVER, 1879-1880. James Abbott McNeill Whistler, American (1834-1903).   Oil on canvas. 20 x 25¾ in. *Emily L. Ainsley Fund. 42.302*
Though most of Whistler's *Nocturnes* were painted in England before 1878, his strong interest in depicting atmospheric conditions and night continued.

GRAND PRIX DAY, 1887. Childe Hassam, American (1859-1935).   Oil on canvas, 24 x 34 in. *Ernest Wadsworth Longfellow Fund. 64.983*
Hassam was known to paint several versions of a favorite subject.

AT THE OPERA, 1879. Mary Cassatt, American (1845-1926).   Oil on canvas. 32 x 26 in. *Charles Henry Hayden Fund. 10.35*

THE DAUGHTERS OF EDWARD D. BOIT, 1882. John Singer Sargent, American (1856-1925). Oil on canvas, 87 x 87 in. *Gift of Mary Louisa Boit, Florence D. Bo[?]* *Jane Hubbard Boit, and Julia Overing Boit, in memory of their father. 19.124* Like Copley and Stuart, Sargent typifies Boston. However, in this unconventiona[?] portrait of the four daughters of his close friend, Edward Boit, Sargent's profound admiration of the high sophistication of Velásquez's work is evident.

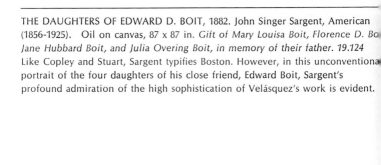

A CUP OF TEA, 1880. Mary Cassatt, American (1845-1926). Oil on canvas. 25½ x 36½ in. *Maria Hopkins Fund. 42.178* Represented are the artist's sister, Lydia, on the left with a friend at their summer villa in Marly-le-Roi.

THE POOR MAN'S STORE, 1885. John Frederick Peto, American (1854-1907). Oil on canvas and wood. 35½ x 25½ in. *M. and M. Karolik Collection 62.278* One of four paintings in the museum's collection by this unique trompe l'oeil painter.

OLD MODELS, 1892. William Michael Harnett, American (1848-1892). Oil on canvas. 54 x 28 in. *Charles Henry Hayden Fund. 39.761* Perhaps Harnett's last painting and certainly one of his greatest, it has also been known as *The Old Cupboard and the Old Cupboard Door.*

PIGEONS, 1910. John Sloan, American (1871-1951). Oil on canvas. 26 x 32 in. *Charles Henry Hayden Fund. 35.52* The pigeon flyers in New York City provided Sloan with a curious entertainment. In a letter dated 1935 he states, "My back windows looked out on the roofs of old tenements on 24th Street. Incidents observed from my back windows furnished me with much material for painting and etching of this period 1905-1911."

DRUG STORE, 1927. Edward Hopper, American (1882-1967). Oil on canvas. 29 x 40 in. *Bequest of John T. Spaulding. 48.564*
Typically devoid of embellishment but rather direct, bold, and lonely in character, this painting is one of three in the collection by Hopper.

REGLER CHURCH, 1930. Lyonel Charles Feininger, American (1871-1956). Oil on canvas. 50 x 40¼ in. *Charles Henry Hayden Fund. 57.198*
This medieval church was so called after the Regler family of Erfurt.

ANNA CHRISTINA, 1967. Andrew Wyeth, American (born 1907). Tempera on masonite, 21½ x 23½ in. *Gift of Amanda K. Berls. 1970.250*
This portrait of Christina Olson was painted shortly before her death in the Olsons' house, which has now been made a museum.

DEPARTMENT OF PRINTS AND DRAWINGS

"Prints by the millions have fluttered into the world during the past five hundred years. Even dullards and impenitent scapegraces have made them as well as creative geniuses, and there is no aspect of dignity, pathos or comedy of human life which they have not tried to express. A well endowed print room might truthfully be likened to a Gargantuan picture book of western civilization." (Henry P. Rossiter, Curator, 1937, at the time of the fiftieth anniversary of the Department of Prints and Drawings.)

Few, if any, large print rooms have a realistic idea of how many pieces they own, and certainly they have no leisure in which to count them. The Department of Prints and Drawings, founded in 1887, estimates that it now has half a million prints, drawings, watercolors, illustrated books, and photographs of American and European origin, dating from the fifteenth century to the present day. In 1897 the Gray Collection of prints was unexpectedly transferred to its rightful owner, Harvard University. At that time the foundation of the Print Room was laid when the first curator, Sylvester R. Koehler, purchased some 23,000 prints collected by Henry F. Sewall, a New York merchant. Sewall's intent, rare for an American collector of his time, was to represent the whole field of printmaking with examples by both major and minor masters from the beginnings through the eighteenth century.

THE LETTER, 1891. Mary Cassatt, American, 1845-1926. Drypoint and aquatint, printed in color. 16 x 11½ in. *Gift of William Emerson and Charles Henry Hayden Fund. 41.803*
Mary Cassatt's set of ten color prints in the museum collection is an outstanding example of printmaking in color. The unusual perspective, the clear colors, and the decorative patterns reflect the influence of Japanese woodblock prints.

The initial broad representation of old master prints has been continued under the guidance of five curators: Koehler (1887-1899), Emil Richter (1905-1912), Fitzroy Carrington (1913-1921), Henry P. Rossiter (1923-1967), and Eleanor A. Sayre (1967-present). Their collective aim from the beginning has been to seek works of quality in the finest possible impressions, as well as to widen the scope of the collection. Throughout they have had the help of patrons of the department such as Francis Bullard and his family, who made important gifts of objects as well as a substantial bequest for the purchase of prints.

Probably the single greatest strength of the collection is the availability in one place of not only a single impression but, for many artists and periods, multiple impressions of a print, permitting the student, scholar, or collector an unequaled method of learning by comparison. A number of preparatory drawings for prints have also been acquired. The department reference library, which includes oeuvre, sales and exhibition catalogues, books on technique, and facsimiles of old master prints and drawings, and the technical collection of original copperplates, woodblocks, and lithographic stones, is an important aid to the study of prints.

The Italian fifteenth century engravings are the most outstanding group owned in this country. Among them are a complete set of the broad manner *Prophets* in the first state, the only complete impression of the large *Judgment Hall of Pilate*, and a charming, unique impression of a Ferrarese *Annunciation*. The print room is also strong in northern engravings of the same period, owning the single known impression of the small *Garden of Love*, by the Master of the Gardens of Love, a "Queen" by the Master of the Playing Cards, and a pair of enchanting drypoints (one of them unique) by the Master of the Amsterdam Cabinet. A hand-colored copy of the first book illustrated by engravings, Colard Mansion's 1476 edition of Boccaccio, *De la ruyne des nobles hommes et femmes*, printed in Bruges, is the outstanding rare book of this period.

The Dürer collection is extremely rich, not only in fine engravings, etchings, drypoints, and woodcuts but also in its wealth of comparative impressions. Without borrowing from other sources, a major exhibition honoring the five-hundredth anniversary of the artist's birth was held in 1971. Other strengths are a magnificent set of Duvet's *Apocalypse* and the collection of chiaroscuro woodcuts by such men as Ugo da Carpi, Vicentino, Andreani, Goltzius, Baldung, and Weiditz, frequently represented in multiple impressions. Greatly enlarged by the bequest of W. G. Russell Allen's collection, this area spans the seventeenth and eighteenth centuries as well, including an extraordinarily complete and rich group of Zanettis.

As in other periods, the seventeenth century printmakers, both eminent and less well known, are well represented, but the etchings of the Lorraine mannerist Bellange constitute a unique part of the collection. Almost all of his subjects are here, many in more than one impression. Ornament prints and books span the centuries and include sixteenth century Italian woodcut lace designs, seventeenth century Spanish calligraphy, and a wealth of eighteenth century material, from Pillement etchings to watercolor patterns for embroidery and *mise-en-cartes* for weaving fabrics. The print room has an especially fine collection of prints by the three Tiepolos and by Canaletto. Among the odd rarities is a complete set of Alexander Cozens' "Blot Prints" together with his explanatory text.

The department was very early interested in acquiring fine Goyas and through two major purchases in 1951 and 1973 now owns some 120 trial proofs for the various series, a set of the *Caprichos* bound for the artist, and an impression of the rare *Giant*, as well as a number of drawings. Two other artists for whose trial proofs the department is known are Turner and Constable.

It is also rich in nineteenth century lithography. The collection ranges from the early experiments of German professionals and English amateurs through the great prints of Daumier, Delacroix, Géricault, Manet, Degas, Toulouse-Lautrec, Gauguin, Redon, Bonnard, and Vuillard, and includes posters by various great designers such as Steinlen, Mucha, and Will Bradley.

The technical manuals of early lithography were the bequest of the first curator, Koehler, who was deeply interested in methods and technique. For this reason he also secured from living American artists trial proofs of different states of their work, often on a variety of papers. Another interesting dimension was added to the collection by Rossiter's acquisition of a large collection of the work of the English illustrators of the 1860's formed by Harold G. Hartley. It includes drawings, wood blocks, and annotated proofs, as well as autograph letters.

The department has always been interested in contemporary printmaking, but it was not until the bequest of funds by Lee M. Friedman in 1959 that a consistent policy of buying became possible. By then, much that was desirable had become the classic prints of the twentieth century. Nevertheless, the department has a number of fine prints by Matisse, Villon, Munch, Kollwitz, and the German expressionists and is fortunate to own Picasso's complete "Vollard Suite." It has also been acquiring the work both of major contemporary printmakers such as Rauschenberg, Johns, Ruscha, and Dine and of lesser known artists.

The drawing and watercolor collection of about 25,000 examples ranges from Lorenzo di Credi to Willem de Kooning. The most important large groups are by Blake, Tiepolo, Millet, Homer, Prendergast, Sargent, and the great M. and M. Karolik Collection of American Drawings and Watercolors, 1800-1875, comprising some 3,000 works. The bequest of Forsyth Wickes, which includes seventy-nine eighteenth century French drawings and watercolors, has considerably enriched the collection. The drawings of major artists such as Dürer, Rembrandt, Goya, Daumier, and Picasso are also represented in the collection.

Books illustrated by printmakers have been considered an integral part of the print collection. The rare book collection now comprises about 5,000 illustrated volumes, ranging from the fifteenth century to the present. The single most important addition was the bequest of William A. Sargent of eighteenth and early nineteenth century French books, as well as a small book purchase fund.

The museum has a small but growing collection of original photographs. The two most important groups are the Southworth and Hawes daguerreotypes and the Stieglitz photographs. Through funds provided by the Polaroid Foundation it has been possible to purchase works by contemporary photographers. The collection of nineteenth and early twentieth century photographers such as Gertrude Käsebier, Hill and Adamson, Frederick Evans, and Alvin Langdon Coburn has been augmented by individual donors.

Some thirty years ago the department pioneered in setting up a laboratory for paper conservation under Francis W. Dolloff. It was a necessity for a collection this size and has also served both private collectors and other museums.

The department's exhibitions change on a regular basis. Each year it arranges a number of exhibitions from various parts of the collection in its six galleries and organizes one special exhibition with a catalogue. Material not on exhibition may be seen at the Print Study Room, Tuesday through Friday between 1 and 4:30. Appointments are requested.

Some exhibitions organized by the department, which had catalogues, are listed below:

The Artist and the Book 1860-1960 (1961)

M. and M. Karolik Collection of Drawings and Watercolors, 1800-1875 (1962)

Boston Museum Bulletin, 65, no. 341, 1967, serves as the catalogue to an exhibition of prints and drawings acquired by Henry P. Rossiter, curator from 1923 to 1967

Rembrandt: Experimental Etcher (1969)

Albrecht Dürer: Master Printmaker (1971)

Camille Pissarro, the Impressionist Printmaker (1973)

Private Realities, Recent American Photography (1974)

Edgar Degas: The Reluctant Impressionist (1974)

The Changing Image: Prints by Francisco Goya (1974)

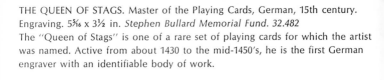

THE QUEEN OF STAGS. Master of the Playing Cards, German, 15th century.
Engraving. 5⅚₆ x 3½ in. *Stephen Bullard Memorial Fund. 32.482*
The "Queen of Stags" is one of a rare set of playing cards for which the artist
was named. Active from about 1430 to the mid-1450's, he is the first German
engraver with an identifiable body of work.

THE SMALL GARDEN OF LOVE. Master of the Gardens of Love, Netherlandish,
active 1440-1450. Engraving. 3⅚₆ x 7¾ in. *Katherine Eliot Bullard Fund. 65.594*
The museum's *Small Garden of Love* is the only surviving impression. The artist,
active about 1440-50, was undoubtedly a goldsmith of Burgundian origin who
came under the influence of Jan van Eyck. He was also the first to introduce
scenes from daily life in his prints.

TWO GENTLEMEN IN A LANDSCAPE. Anonymous, North Italian (Veronese),
ca. 1470-1485. Engraving. 6 x 7⅜ in. *Samuel Putnam Avery Fund. 21.10594*
This anonymous engraver has skillfully recorded for posterity the fashions of the
times.

THE PLANET MARS, ca. 1465. Attributed to Baccio Baldini, Florentine, 15th century. Engraving. 12⅞ x 8⅝ in. *James Fund. 15.1339*
A series of early Florentine engravings illustrates the seven planets and their influence on mankind. In this print, Mars encircles the earth and oversees the various operations of war. Two signs of the Zodiac, the Scorpion and the Ram, form the wheels of his chariot.

SAINT JEROME IN PENITENCE, ca. 1465-1470. Anonymous, Master of the Vienna Passion, Florentine. Engraving, hand colored. 9¾ x 6¼ in. *Stephen Bullard Memorial Fund. 31.987*
This is the only known impression of a very early Florentine engraving, delicately hand colored in ochre, green, and red.

MARTE·E·SEGNO·MALCULINO·POSTO·NEL·QUINTO·CIELO·MOLTO·CALDO·SOCOSO·SA·QUESTE·P
ROPRIETA·DAMARE·MILITIA·BAT·TAGLIE·ET·UCCIZIONI·MALICNO·DIZORDINATO·DEMETALLI·UA·IL
FERRO·DEGLI·QMORI·LACOLLERA·DETEMPLI·LA·ETATE·ELDI·SUO·E·IL·MARTEDI·COLLA·PRIMA·HORA·S
I·ET·Z·Z·ELA·SUA·NOTTE·EI·LSABATO·EISUO·AMICO·E·ILSOLE·EL·NIMICO·GIOVE·A·DUE·AB
ITATIONI·ELDI·LARIETE·E·LANOT·TE·LOSCORPIONE·LAVITA·OVERO·ESATASIONE·SUA·E
CARRICORNO·LASUA·MORTE·OVERO·ESATA·HUMILIASIONE·I·ILCANCRO·ET·VA
E·I·Z·SENGNI·IN·18·APPINATI·MESI·COMINCANDO·NELLO·SCORFIONE·IN·NU
N·MESE·E·MESO·CIOE·4·5·DI·IMSENGNO·40·MINUTI·PERDI·ET·PERORA·VN
MINUTO·ET·4·SECONDI

PIETA. Anonymous, South Germany, active about 1460-1480. Woodcut, hand colored. 14⅞ x 10⅞ in. *William Francis Warden Fund. 53.359*
This crudely powerful woodcut, hand colored with transparent washes of red, ochre, and green, is a good example of these now exceptionally rare German prints that were originally intended as inexpensive substitutes for paintings. They were used as devotional images in homes or chapels and were often pasted into the covers of missals or bound into books.

TRIUMPH OVER DESPAIR from "THE ART OF DYING," ca. 1450. Master E. S., German, active about 1440-1468. Engraving. 3⅝ x 2¾ in. *Katherine Eliot Bullard Fund. 1970.23*
The *Triumph of Despair* is one of eleven engravings made by the Master E. S. to illustrate the *Ars Moriendi* (The Art of Dying). In this medieval treatise the devil either successfully tempts a dying man or is defeated by Christ and his heavenly court, who give strength to the patient. Here, an angel shows him four famous reformed personages from the New Testament, Saul, the repentant thief, Mary Magdalene, and Saint Peter.

THE ANNUNCIATION. Anonymous, Ferrarese, ca. 1470-1480. Engraving. 7½ x 10 in. *1951 Purchase Fund. 54.576*
A unique impression, this delicate engraving shows the characteristic regional style of the Ferrarese school as exemplified by the painter Francesco del Cossa (ca. 1435-ca. 1477) and the frescoes at the Schifanoia Palace.

GIOVANNI BOCCACCIO, *De la ruyne des nobles hommes et femmes*, 1476. Published by Colard Mansion, Bruges. Illustration shown: "Boccaccio writing down the story of Adam and Eve," by an anonymous Flemish engraver called the Master of the Boccaccio Illustrations. Engraving, hand colored. 8¼ x 6¼ in. *Maria Antoinette Evans Fund. 32.458*

The Bruges edition of Boccaccio's tale of the downfall of famous men and women (some legendary, some real) was the first printed book to be illustrated with engravings. The museum's copy is one of three known examples in which all nine engraved illustrations have been pasted in, and the only copy in which all engravings have been colored by hand, giving the intended effect of illuminated miniatures.

MOTHER WITH TWO CHILDREN AND A BLANK SHIELD. BEARDED MAN WITH A BLANK SHIELD. Master of the Amsterdam Cabinet, German, active last quarter of the 15th century. Two drypoints. Each 3¾ x 2⅞ in. *Katherine Eliot Bullard Fund. 66.375, 66.376*

The master is so named because most of his prints can be found in the print room of the Rijksmuseum, Amsterdam. The Boston Museum's *Mother with Two Children* is a unique impression, and the *Bearded Man* is one of five examples. The artist's direct, lively observation of the real world and his technique influenced the work of Albrecht Dürer.

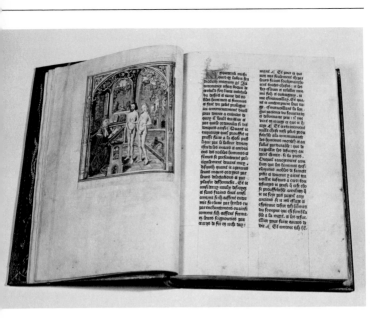

ONE-MASTED SHIP. Master W♣, Netherlandish, active ca. 1465-1485. Engraving. 6¾6 x 5¼ in. *Gift of Mrs. T. Jefferson Coolidge and Maria Antoinette Evans Fund. M 31541*
This brilliant, strongly inked impression belongs to a rare series of eight prints representing one and two-masted vessels, probably the first marine prints. The artist, known only by his monogram and sign, is thought to have been attached to the court of Charles the Bold at Antwerp.

VIRGIN AND CHILD IN A COURTYARD. Martin Schongauer, German, about 1450-1491. Engraving. 6⅝ x 4¾ in. *Harvey D. Parker Collection. 97.1116*
The painter Schongauer's clarity of graphic composition brought a refinement to engraving hitherto unknown in Northern Europe. Albrecht Dürer attempted to visit the painter-printmaker in Colmar on his student travels but arrived shortly after Schongauer's death.

STAG BROWSING. Master of the Beheading of John the Baptist, Italian, active ca. 1500-1525. Engraving, 7⅜ x 5¾6 in. *Stephen Bullard, Horatio Greenough Curtis, George Peabody Gardner, and Otis Norcross funds. 49.331*
Only four prints are attributed to this anonymous Milanese artist, whose feeling for animals and skill in delineating them was unusual for his time. To achieve a soft, tonal effect, the engraver employed a delicate stipple technique.

CENTAUR ATTACKED BY TWO MEN. Master I. A. M. of Zwolle, Netherlandish, active about 1485.   Engraving. 5⅞ x 8¾ in. *Harriet Otis Cruft Fund. 32.532*
The Master I. A. M. of Zwolle's lively composition is enforced by his jagged contour lines and animated drapery modeling. Mythological subjects such as this were rarely treated by Northern European printmakers in the fifteenth century.

THE BATTLE OF THE SEA GODS (left half of frieze), ca. 1485-1488. Andrea Mantegna, Italian, 1431-1506.   Engraving. 11⅝ x 17 in. *Bequest of Francis Bullard in memory of Stephen Bullard, 1913. M24555*
Printed in a soft brown ink and shaded in the style of his pen drawings, this engraving conveys the skill and graphic brilliance of Mantegna, who mastered the difficult use of the burin with the same distinction as the pen.

SELF-PORTRAIT OF THE ARTIST AND HIS WIFE. Israhel van Meckenem, German, ca. 1445-1503. Engraving. 5⅛ x 6⅞ in. *Harriet Otis Cruft Fund. M28128*
Israhel van Meckenem has been known primarily as a copyist of works by other artists. However, he was also extremely inventive, creating many engravings of fifteenth century daily life. This double portrait is the first printed portrait of a known sitter.

MAXIMILIAN I's "WEISSKUNIG" (Liechtenstein Codex G), "Presentation of the Book to the Emperor." Woodcut, proof impression by Hans Burgkamair, German, 1473-1531. Facing title page made by a seventeenth century owner of the Codex, with additional notes in various hands. *William Francis Warden Fund. 57.40*
The *Weisskunig* (White King) is a book commissioned by Maximilian I, Holy Roman Emperor from 1508 to 1519, wherein his personal exploits, education, and battles are illustrated with woodcuts as an epic glorification of his reign. As the book was never completed, the museum's copy is actually an album of proofs for the woodcuts and has manuscript notes in various hands, including Maximilian's.

HEAD OF A YOUTH. Lorenzo di Credi, Italian, 1459(?)-1537. Silverpoint, heightened with white on gray, prepared paper. 8¹³⁄₁₆ x 7⅝ in. *Gift of Dr. Denman W. Ross. 17.592*
This portrait exhibits an almost perfect combination of subject and treatment. The delicate yet incisive silverpoint lines are innately suited to delineate the sensitive features of this winsome young man.

PORTRAIT OF EMPEROR MAXIMILIAN I, 1520. Lucas van Leyden, Netherlandish, 1494-1533. Engraving and etching. 10⅛ x 7⁹⁄₁₆ in. *William Francis Warden Fund. 48.3*
In his portrait of Maximilian, Lucas' use of a combination of etching and engraving was an innovation. He first etched the composition and then completed the shading and details of head and garment with a refined engraved line The model for this portrait was Albrecht Dürer's 1518 woodcut of the emperor.

CHRIST CARRYING THE CROSS. Anonymous, Milanese, ca. 1500. Woodcut, hand colored. 21¾ x 16½ in. *Katherine Eliot Bullard Fund. 63.2668*
This striking, hand-colored woodcut is from the museum's outstanding collection of early Italian prints. It contrasts markedly to the only other contemporary impression, printed in grayish black ink and highly restored.

SATURN, Ugo da Carpi, Italian, ca. 1455-1523. Chiaroscuro woodcut, 12⅝ x 17⅜ in. *Bequest of W. G. Russell Allen. 64.1110*
Ugo da Carpi was one of the earliest Italian printmakers to simulate the effect of wash drawings by means of color woodcuts conceived in terms of light and shade rather than line.

A WITCHES' SABBATH, 1510. Hans Baldung-Grien, German, 1484/5-1545. Chiaroscuro woodcut. 14⅞ x 10¼ in. *Bequest of W. G. Russell Allen. 69.1064*
Except for two engravings by Albrecht Dürer, Baldung-Grien's *A Witches' Sabbath* of 1510 is one of the earliest Northern European representations of witchcraft produced independently of book illustration.

VIRGIN AND CHILD IN A ROUNDEL ABOVE A ROCKY LANDSCAPE, ca. 1515.
Albrecht Dürer, German, 1471-1528. Woodcut. 5⅞ x 3⅞ in. *Centennial Gift of
Landon T. Clay. 68.197*
Dürer designed the two seemingly unrelated images on one woodblock. The
result was highly unconventional for his day but is nevertheless successful.

MOUNTAIN LANDSCAPE WITH FIR TREES, ca. 1517-1520. Albrecht Altdorfer,
German, ca. 1480-1538. Etching. 4⅝ x 6½ in. *Horatio Greenough Curtis Fund.
27.1292*
Altdorfer was one of the first of many German artists who looked to their
surrounding landscape, the Danube River valley, for their subjects. They found
the spontaneity of line afforded by the newly developed technique of etching to
be most suitable for their treatment of landscape.

FARMBUILDINGS WITH POLLARDED TREE. Fra Bartolommeo, Italian, 1472-1517.
Pen and brown ink. 11¼ x 8½ in. *Francis Bartlett Fund. 58.1*
Landscapes were an unusual subject for fifteenth century Florentine draughtsmen.
When a rare album full of Fra Bartolommeo drawings such as this came up at
auction in 1957, the museum was fortunate in being able to acquire a double-
sided sheet whose delicate sketches from nature evoke a sun-drenched Tuscan
hillside.

THE HOLY TRINITY, 1515. Albrecht Dürer, German, 1471-1528. Pen and bistre.
11¾ x 8⅞₆ in. *1931 Purchase Fund and Anna Mitchell Richards Fund. 36.418*
Dürer's drawing of 1515 is a revision in his mature style of the 1511 woodcut of
the same subject.

SAINT SEBASTIAN. Jacopo de' Barbari, Italian, ca. 1460/70-by 1516.   Engraving.
8¹¹⁄₁₆ x 6⅜ in. *Stephen Bullard Memorial Fund. 38.1742*
One of the more fruitful exchanges of artistic ideas seems to have taken place
between the Venetian de' Barbari and his German contemporary Albrecht Dürer,
who twice visited Venice. Since most of de' Barbari's engravings are undated, it
is often uncertain as to who influenced whom. This fine print is dated toward
1510, and its careful, delicate modeling of the flesh shows the artist's
indebtedness to Dürer's engravings, in particular the *Adam and Eve* of 1504.

SAINT JEROME SEATED BY A POLLARD WILLOW, 1512. Albrecht Dürer,
German, 1471-1528.   Drypoint. 8⅜ x 7¼ in. *Anna Mitchell Richards Fund.
37.1296*
So rich and coloristic an impression of a Dürer drypoint is rare, for such is the
nature of the medium that the burr of the lines scratched on a copper plate
wears off after only a few printings.

THE WOMAN CLOTHED WITH THE SUN. Jean Duvet, French, 1485-after 1561. Engraving from *The Apocalypse* (1561). 11⅝ x 8⅛ in. *1951 Purchase Fund. 51.715* The museum owns a fine set of the twenty-four plates of Duvet's *Apocalypse*. These intricate conceptions magnificently picture the visionary writings of Saint John, as influenced by the religious upheavals of the Reformation and Counter-Reformation.

THE THREE MARYS AT THE TOMB. Jacques Bellange, French, active 1602-1617. Etching. 17¼ x 11⅜ in. *Otis Norcross Fund. 40.119* The style and courtly elegance of the three women surprised by the angel at the empty tomb of Christ are typical of this highly individual, mannerist etcher from Lorraine. Bellange is represented by almost his entire printed oeuvre, in part from the collection of Robert-Dumesnil, the nineteenth century collector and cataloguer of French prints.

RAZULLO AND CUCURUCU. Jacques Callot, French, 1592-1635. Etching from the set *Balli di Sfessania*. 2¹³⁄₁₆ x 3⅝ in. *William Simes Fund. 29.1884*

THE HANGING TREE. Jacques Callot, French, 1592-1635. Etching from *Les Misères et les malheurs de la guerre* (Paris, 1633). 3³⁄₁₆ x 7⁵⁄₁₆ in. *Katherine Eliot Bullard Fund. 1970.307* The prolific Callot treated many subjects. These two prints illustrate how diverse these can be. One shows a fantastically costumed, cavorting pair from Italian comedy, while the other is a humanitarian outcry against the grotesque tortures of war. The inscription refers to the bodies as "hanging from the tree like unhappy fruit."

Razullo. Cucurucu. 19

ROCKY LANDSCAPE WITH A CHURCH TOWER. Hercules Seghers, Netherlandish 1589/90-1639/40. Etching, printed in blue-green on paper with pink ground, colored with olive-green wash. 5⅛ x 7⅜ in. *Purchased from the Kate D. Griswold, Ernest Longfellow, Jessie Wilkinson, Katherine Eliot Bullard, and M. and M. Karolik funds. 1973.208*
The early seventeenth century Dutch painter Hercules Seghers was responsible for the most inventive and expressive printmaking experiments of his time. His use of colored inks, colored grounds, and hand-applied color usually produced a printed image that was essentially unique rather than repeatable. The present image with its unearthly pink sky is characteristic of Seghers' transformation in mood of Breughel's conception of the mountain landscape.

WATCHDOG SLEEPING IN HIS KENNEL, ca. 1633. Rembrandt van Rijn, Netherlandish, 1606-1669. Pen, bistre, and gallnut ink. 5⅝ x 6⅝ in. *J. H. and E. A. Payne Fund. 56.519*
This is a fine example of one of Rembrandt's many direct, spontaneous notations from the daily life about him.

STUDIES OF A RIVER GOD. Peter Paul Rubens, Netherlandish, 1577-1640. Black chalk on green buff paper, squared for transfer. 16¼ x 9⁷⁄₁₆ in. *Frances Draper Colburn Fund. 20.813*
This vigorous study by the great Flemish Baroque painter has been squared for transfer to a larger format. The project for which it is a study, whether painting or tapestry cartoon, has not been identified.

THE GOOD SAMARITAN. Rembrandt van Rijn, Netherlandish, 1606-1669. Etching. 9⅝ x 8 in. *Stephen Bullard Memorial Fund. 43.1341*
This down-to-earth version of the Biblical narrative teems with circumstantial, anecdotal detail matched by a refinement and complication of line utterly unlike the bold economy that characterizes Rembrandt's later prints. It is only in fine, early impressions like this one that one experiences the full range of tones and effects of illumination that brings order to this diversity of detail.

THE AGONY IN THE GARDEN, ca. 1657. Rembrandt van Rijn, Netherlandish, 1606-1669. Etching and drypoint. 4⅞₆ x 3⅜₆ in. *Katherine Eliot Bullard Fund. 1973.288*
One of the smallest of Rembrandt's compositions and yet one of the most monumental, this print is very dependent on the velvety drypoint accents that are quickly worn away by the pressure of printing. This very rich impression must be one of the earliest and most expressive printed from the plate.

ANNUNCIATION WITH KNEELING ANGEL. Giovanni Battista Tiepolo, Italian, 1696-1770. Pen and bistre over black chalk. 17⅛ x 11¾ in. *Bequest of Mrs. Edward Jackson Holmes, Edward Jackson Holmes Collection. 64.2096*
Giovanni Battista Tiepolo's drawing corresponds in style to his paintings of 1732 and 1733.

SCHERZI DI FANTASIA. Plate IV. Giovanni Battista Tiepolo, Italian, 1696-1770. Etching. 8⅞ x 7¼ in. *George R. Nutter Fund and gift of W. G. Russell Allen.* *45.105*

Tiepolo, fascinated by the occult, magicians and sorcerers, the antique and oriental worlds, youth and old age, life and death, etched the *Scherzi di fantasia* with variety and economy of means, placing them in brilliant Mediterranean sunlight.

THE MILLINERY SHOP, 1791. Giovanni Domenico Tiepolo, Italian, 1729-1804. Pen, gray and brown washes, and yellow watercolor. 11⅜ x 16⅛ in. *William E. Nickerson Fund. 47.2*

Giovanni Domenico Tiepolo had spent nearly half a century on commissioned decorations for palaces and churches when he retired to Venice after 1784 for the remaining twenty years of his life. There he produced a small group of personal and lively comments on the contemporary Venetian scene, as in this delightful drawing.

"THE WOUNDED ONE" from PAPILLONERIES HUMAINES. Charles Germain de Saint-Aubin, French, 1721-1786. Etching. 7⅛ x 10¾ in. *Ellen Page Hall Fund.* *34.589*

The museum owns twelve of these rare and enchanting prints in which butterflies play human roles. Their rococo fantasy is fabricated of gossamer grace and a delicately barbed Gallic wit.

FOUR STUDIES OF A WOMAN. Jean-Antoine Watteau, French, 1684-1721.
Red, black, and white chalk on tan paper. 13½ x 9½ in. *Forsyth Wickes
Collection. 65.2610*
Watteau filled many notebooks with sketches and drawings that he then used in
his paintings. The woman in the upper left appears in two paintings: *The Game
of Love* (London) and *Assembly in a Park* (Berlin).

PORTRAIT OF MARIE ANTOINETTE, 1777. Jean François Janinet, French, 1752-
1814. Color aquatint with separate border, gilt in border added by hand.
16½ x 12½ in. *Bequest of John B. How. 44.794*
Successful in its attempt to recreate a painting, this is an unusually beautiful
early color print.

"JERSEY NANNY," 1748. John Greenwood, American, 1721-1792.   Mezzotint.
9¾ x 7¾ in. *Gift of Henry Lee Shattuck. 1971.715*
Greenwood painted formal portraits, but had an eye for the world around him.
This print of a coarse-featured, buxom working woman was advertised in the
Boston Gazette, December 20, 1748, as a "Portrait of Ann Arnold . . .who
generally goes by the name of Jersey Nanny."

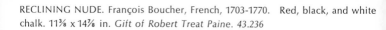

RECLINING NUDE. François Boucher, French, 1703-1770.   Red, black, and white chalk. 11⅜ x 14⅞ in. *Gift of Robert Treat Paine. 43.236*

TWO VIEWS OF A SLEEPING CHILD. Jean-Michel Moreau, French, 1741-1814. Pen, brush, and gray wash. 4 x 5¹⁵⁄₁₆ in. (each). *Forsyth Wickes Collection. 65.2592 (to right), 65.2593 (to left)*
Moreau's *Two Views of a Sleeping Child* have been identified as the artist's daughter, Catherine Françoise, born in 1765. The drawings have been part of several renowned collections, including that of the Goncourt brothers in the nineteenth century.

STANDING NUDE, ca. 1814. Pierre-Paul Prud'hon, French, 1758-1823. Charcoal heightened with white chalk on blue paper. 24 x 13¾ in. *Forsyth Wickes Collection. 65.2598*
During his 1884-89 sojourn in Italy Prud'hon was deeply impressed with the neo-classic sculpture of Canova as well as the drawings of Leonardo and Corregio. These influences may be seen in this drawing, one of at least three studies of a favorite model, Marguerite.

VIEW ON THE LAGOON or CAPRICCIO WITH A HOUSE AND TOWER ON THE LAGOON. Antonio Canale (called Canaletto), Italian, 1697-1798. Pencil, pen, bistre, and gray wash over ruled pencil. 8⅜ x 12⁷⁄₁₆ in. *Arthur Mason Knapp Fund. 48.1322*
Landscape painter, draughtsman, and etcher, Canaletto recorded the beauty of eighteenth century Venice. His studies range from the photographically accurate to elaborate imaginative designs. In this drawing there is a remarkable feeling of space filled with sunlight and air.

THE PRISONS, PLATE VI, ca. 1745. Giovanni Battista Piranesi, Italian, 1720-1778. Etching, first state. 21⅜ x 15¾ in. *Stephen Bullard Memorial Fund. 25.422*
Piranesi's etchings of prisons surpass in grandeur the baroque opera sets that inspired them. Only an imaginative architect could have designed the lofty stairways, the endless arches, and the hanging chains of these visionary designs.

LANDSCAPE FROM "A NEW METHOD OF ASSISTING THE INVENTION IN DRAWING ORIGINAL COMPOSITIONS OF LANDSCAPE." Alexander Cozens, English, 1717-1786. Aquatint. 9⅜ x 12⅜ in. *Horatio Greenough Curtis Fund. 30.1430*
His contemporaries derisively termed Cozens "The Blotmaster General to the Town," in reference to his making use of accidental conformations of ink as the basis for landscape compositions. The sixteen aquatints of this series are prophetically modern in their freedom and abstraction.

CHRIST AND THE WOMAN TAKEN IN ADULTERY, ca. 1805. William Blake,
English, 1757-1827.   Watercolor. 14 x 14⅛ in. *Gift by subscription, 1890. 90.110*
The museum owns thirty-three Blake watercolors representing his visual
translations of Milton's *Paradise Lost* and *Comus: A Mask*, Shakespeare's plays,
and subjects taken from the Old and New Testaments. Before their acquisition by
the museum in 1890 many of these works had been part of the first important
Blake exhibition, held in London in 1876.

THE GIANT (COLOSSUS). Francisco Goya y Lucientes, Spanish, 1746-1828.
Aquatint. 11¼ x 8¼ in., about 1818. *Katherine Eliot Bullard Fund. 65.1296*
The museum's impression of Goya's enigmatic and powerful *Giant* is one of two
known impressions of the first state. The print reflects Goya's absolute mastery
of the aquatint process.

[VILE ADVANTAGE]. Francisco Goya y Lucientes, Spanish, 1746-1828. Etching, unique proof for *Los Desastres de la guerra* (ca. 1810-1820). 5¾₁₆ x 7⅝₁₆ in. *1951 Purchase Fund. 51.1697*
This, the only known impression, represents an outstanding group of some seventy-five working proofs for the "Disasters of War." These are the rare and beautiful impressions printed by or for Goya himself. The series was not published until 1863, thirty-five years after Goya's death.

PEDRO ROMERO MATANDO Á TORO PARADO (Pedro Romero killing a bull he has subdued). Francisco Goya y Lucientes, Spanish, 1746-1828. Red chalk drawing for plate 30 of *La Tauromaquia* (by 1816). 7¾ x 11⅛ in. *Frederick J. Kennedy Memorial Foundation. 1973.696*
The museum is fortunate in owning a number of drawings by Goya that are studies for prints. Goya's somewhat personal history of bullfighting is illustrated by the daring and singular exploits of individual bullfighters, such as this.

THE GUILLON-LETHIÈRE FAMILY, 1815. Jean Auguste Dominique Ingres, French, 1780-1867. Graphite. 10¹⁵₁₆ x 8¹¹₁₆ in. *Maria Antoinette Evans Fund. 26.45*
In this superb example of Ingres' Roman portraiture the cool finesse of his pencil glows under the contagious charm of this handsome young family.

HENRY, EARL OF BATHHURST. John Singleton Copley, American, 1737-1815.
Black chalk, heightened with white on gray-blue paper. 26 x 19½ in.
M. and M. Karolik Collection. 41.683
The museum owns a number of Copley's drawings, most of which are for
paintings executed in England. This life-sized study of the Lord High
Chancellor for the painting *The Death of the Earl of Chatham* (1779-1781) is
reminiscent of his earlier, more direct American portraits.

SPRING BLESSING. Anonymous folk artist, American, late 18th century.
Pen and watercolor. 7¹³⁄₁₆ x 12⁵⁄₁₆ in. *M. and M. Karolik Collection. 50.3839*

ROBERT OWEN — A STUDY FROM LIFE, 1833. Rembrandt Peale, American,
1778-1860.   Black crayon on light brown paper. 15⁷⁄₁₆ x 11⅞ in. *M. and M.
Karolik Collection. 56.398*
A refined, early Pennsylvania fraktur drawing and the sensitive portrait of an
early social reformer represent the some 3,000 American drawings and watercolors of the Karolik Collection.

BISHOP THOMAS M. CLARKE OF RHODE ISLAND. Firm of Southworth and
Hawes, Boston. Daguerreotype, 19th century, quarter plate. 8½ x 6½ in.
*Gift of Edward Southworth Hawes in memory of his father, Josiah Johnson
Hawes. 43.1391*
The museum is fortunate in owning 112 daguerreotypes by the Boston firm of
Southworth and Hawes, the most distinuished American portrait daguerreo-
typists of the time.

DAPPLED DRAUGHT HORSE BEING SHOD, ca. 1823. Théodore Gericault, French, 1791-1824.   Pencil, gray and brown washes. 6½ x 9⅜ in. *Mary L. Smith Fund.* *59.524*
Warm tonality and powerful modeling of the horse's anatomy characterize this study for the lithograph (Delteil 72).

LE RENDEZ-VOUS DES CHATS. 1868. Edouard Manet, French, 1832-1883. Lithograph. 16¹³⁄₁₆ x 13 in. *Gift of W. G. Russell Allen. 32.472*

LE VENTRE LÉGISLATIF. Honoré Daumier, French, 1808-1879.   Lithograph (L'Association Mensuelle, 1834). Image, 11 x 17 in. *Bequest of William P. Babcock. B4299*
Through his lithographs, Daumier became one of the great voices of republican opposition to the government of Louis-Philippe. In *Le Ventre législatif* he has satirized those figures on the benches of the Chamber of Deputies who had shown singular loyalty to the July Monarchy.

STONEHENGE AT DAYBREAK. Joseph Mallord William Turner, English, 1775-1851. Sepia wash. 7⅝ x 10⅚ in. *Gift of Miss Ellen T. Bullard. 59.795*
The museum's extensive collection of Turner's *Liber Studiorum* (Book of Studies) includes the line etchings by Turner and trial proofs and finished mezzotints, as well as the published states. This drawing is a study for an unpublished plate engraved in mezzotint probably by Turner himself.

WOMEN CARRYING FAGGOTS, 1852-1854. Jean François Millet, French, 1814-1875. Black conté crayon. 11⅜ x 18⅞ in. *Gift of Martin Brimmer. 76.437*
Nineteenth century Boston collectors admired the Barbizon School, and through their gifts the museum is rich in Millet's paintings, pastels, and drawings. The sympathy of the artist for the worker is effectively expressed in this drawing where the crayon strokes unify each woman and her burden into one being.

BEGGAR'S FOOTPATH, 1882. Camille Pissarro, French, 1830-1903. Drypoint and aquatint, third state. 6¼ x 4¾ in. *Gift of the Print and Drawing Club. 1971.182*
Lightly incised lines and small delicate flecks of aquatint suggest leafy tree branches and also give this image a dappled, sunlit appearance. Camille Pissarro created prints that fully reflected his Impressionist painterly goals.

THE VIOLINIST, ca. 1879. Hilaire-Germain-Edgar Degas, French, 1834-1917.
Charcoal and white chalk. 18⅞ x 12 in. *William Francis Warden Fund. 58.1263*
Degas' charcoal drawing is a study for the oil painting *The Rehearsal* in the
Frick Collection. The numerous erasures reinforce the assertive contour lines
and heighten the effect of animation. Degas has shown great sensitivity in
depicting the old violinist with bemused expression, who plays endlessly for the
young ballet dancers.

SIMPLON PASS, THE TEASE, 1911. John Singer Sargent, American, 1856-1925.
Watercolor, 15¾ x 20½ in. *Charles Henry Hayden Fund. 12.216*
Influenced by the Impressionists' style, Sargent captures a spontaneous moment
and the play of light in this watercolor of 1911, painted during a visit to
Switzerland. The tease is Rose Marie Ormond, Sargent's niece; her companion
is Miss Polly Barnard.

UMBRELLAS IN THE RAIN (Porte della Paglia, Venice), 1899. Maurice Prendergast, American, 1859-1924.   Watercolor. 13⅝ x 20½ in. *Charles Henry Hayden
Fund. 59.57*
Influenced by his early association with the French Impressionists, Maurice
Prendergast delighted in rendering scenes with shimmering patterns of bright
color. *Umbrellas in the Rain,* one of seventeen Prendergast watercolors in the
museum collection, was painted in Venice during the artist's third visit to Europe
in 1898-99.

ADIRONDACK GUIDE, 1894. Winslow Homer, American, 1836-1910. Watercolo
15 x 21½ in. *Bequest of Alma H. Wadleigh. 47.268*
The bold design and brilliant color of this watercolor painted during a summer
visit to the Adirondacks in 1894 make this one of the finest of Homer's mature
watercolors. The old *Adirondack Guide* is Harvey Holt, whom the artist painted
several times.

THE TERMINAL, NEW YORK, 1892. Alfred Stieglitz, American, 1864-1946.
Photograph. 2⁵⁄₁₆ x 3⅞ in. *Gift of Alfred Stieglitz. 24.1739*
Alfred Stieglitz's gift of twenty-four of his photographs initiated the museum's
photography collection in 1924. In 1950 Miss Georgia O'Keeffe complemented
his gift with a second group of thirty-five photographs by Stieglitz. Together
these groups encompass a period of forty years and provide a major record of
Stieglitz's work.

YOUNG GIRL. Vincent van Gogh, Netherlandish, 1853-1890.   Charcoal, graphite,
brown and black wash, heightened with white. 19⅛ x 10⁵⁄₁₆ in. *William Francis
Warden Fund. 1970.468*
In this drawing, done in the early 1880's, van Gogh has given the childish figure
strength and dignity by bold delineation of form: rubbing, scraping, and
gouging the surface of the tough wove paper.

MELANCHOLY (EVENING), 1896. Edvard Munch, Norwegian, 1863-1944. Woodcut in color. 14⅞ x 17⅞ in. *William Francis Warden Fund. 57.356* Edvard Munch's early woodcuts influenced the style and expressive content of many of the finest twentieth century woodcuts. His use of the natural grain of the woodblock as part of the design was particularly influential. Like many of Munch's early woodcuts, *Melancholy* was printed in a number of subtly varied color combinations.

MANAO TUPAPAU ("Watched by the Spirit of the Dead"), 1893. Paul Gauguin, French, 1848-1903. Color woodcut. 8⅜₁₆ x 20½ in. *Gift of W. G. Russell Allen. 54.1607* Gauguin's handling of the woodblock is well suited to his emphasis on the decorative and exotic. The subtle harmonies of color can only be appreciated in the trial proofs printed by the artist. This impression is an example of such an early printing.

SAILBOATS AT FEHMARN, 1914. Ernst Ludwig Kirchner, German, 1880-1938. Woodcut. 16½ x 15⁷₁₆ in. *Lee M. Friedman Fund. 68.719* In this woodcut by the foremost German Expressionist printmaker the rhythm of the cutting and gouging of the wood contributes powerfully to the total movement of the design.

HEAD AND FIGURE STUDIES, 1906. Pablo Picasso, Spanish, 1881-1973.   Conté
crayon. Sight, 24 x 17⅝ in. *Arthur Tracy Cabot Fund. 63.124*
Picasso's power as a draughtsman is revealed in this study for the oil painting
Two Nudes. The solidly modeled figures and their placement on the page
give this sketch sheet the appearance of a finished composition.

THE BULL, 1945. Pablo Picasso, Spanish, 1881-1973.   Lithographs, third and
eleventh states. 13³⁄₁₆ x 21¼ in. *Lee M. Friedman Fund. 1970.272 and 1970.277*
In the museum collection are six of the eleven states of Picasso's lithograph of
a bull, on which he worked from December 5, 1945, to January 7, 1946. These
proofs demonstrate the process by which a great artist has altered his image by
redrawing, scraping, and erasing. Picasso's final version is a spare abstraction
that is a mere memory of the bull.

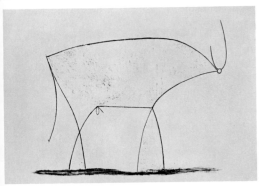

BARN INTERIOR, NO. 1, ca. 1916. Arthur Dove, American, 1880-1946. Charcoal. 21½ x 18½ in. *Anonymous gift. 1972.851*

IN THE PROVINCE. Charles Demuth, American, 1883-1935. Gouache. 23⅛ x 19³⁄₁₆ in. *Anonymous gift in memory of Nathaniel Saltonstall. 67.790*

STANDARD STATION, 1966. Edward Ruscha, American, b. 1937. Color silkscreen. 19½ x 36¾ in. *IGAS Fund. 68.177*
Edward Ruscha's pristine, streamlined *Standard Station* is an ambiguous emblem of our society. It is also one of the finest examples of the revival of silkscreen as an artistic medium in the 1960's.

DAYTONA BEACH from "The Romance of Chrome," 1972. Burke Uzzle, American, b. 1938. Photograph. 10³⁄₁₆ x 12¹⁵⁄₁₆ in. *Polaroid Foundation Purchase Fund. 1973.115*
Burke Uzzle sees the motorcycle, one of the principal icons of American popular culture, surrounded by a haze of romantic glamour.

0 THROUGH 9, 1960. Jasper Johns, American, b. 1930.   Lithograph. 24 x 18 in. *Gift of Lewis P. Cabot. 1970.607*
Jasper Johns' dynamic image, which emphasizes the gestural nature of the act of drawing, is a kind of cubist puzzle in which all of the numbers from 0 through 9 are present but inextricably fused so that the eye cannot isolate individual numbers.

BREAKTHROUGH II, 1965. Robert Rauschenberg, American, b. 1925.   Lithograph. 43¾ x 30 in. *Gift of Lewis P. Cabot. 1970.515*
This work combines the painterly freedom of New York School abstract expressionism with a new vocabulary of photomechanical images drawn from the mass media.

DEPARTMENT OF TEXTILES

Although the Department of Textiles was not established as an independent department until 1930, the assembling of a collection of patterned textiles was an important consideration in the minds of the museum founders. Handsome tapestries, silk weavings, embroideries, and ecclesiastical vestments figured among the works of art lent by the Boston Athenaeum to the Museum of Fine Arts when the museum's first building was opened at Copley Square in 1876. Earlier still, the museum began registering objects for its permanent collection, and it is significant that the second work of art to receive a registration number was a tapestry.

Today the museum's collection of textiles ranks among the great collections of the world, both in terms of the high quality and rarity of individual pieces and as a general collection of representative weavings, embroideries, laces, printed fabrics, and costumes from all parts of the world, ranging in date from the Pharaonic period in Egypt to the present time. Pre-Christian textiles from Egypt are kept in the Egyptian Department, and textiles and costumes from the Far East may be found in the Asiatic Department. The Department of Textiles has charge of all other textile objects from other parts of the world, including tapestries and rugs, ranging in date from the first millennium B.C. in Peru to the present.

The following groups should be listed among the most outstanding holdings. First, the collection of tapestry weavings, which includes fine examples woven in the eastern Mediterranean world in the first millennium of our era as well as the collection of fourteenth, fifteenth, and sixteenth century European tapestries, with important examples from weaving centers in France, Flanders, and Germany. The collection of Peruvian tapestries from the colonial period, ranging from the second half of the sixteenth century through the eighteenth, stands unrivaled as a single collection not only in this country but in Peru as well. French, German, and Italian tapestry weaving of the seventeenth and eighteenth centuries is also well represented. Earlier Peruvian weavings and embroideries, dating from the pre-Christian era through the middle of the sixteenth century, were chosen for beauty of design and workmanship; but incidentally many of the pieces, particularly the collection of embroidered mantles and skirts from the Paracas culture (about 500 to 200 B.C.), are also of the greatest rarity and archaeological importance.

English and continental European embroideries and laces of the fifteenth through nineteenth centuries mark the nucleus of both the Elizabeth Day McCormick Collection, acquired 1943-53, and the collection of Mrs. Philip Lehman, which was presented in Mrs. Lehman's memory by her husband in 1938. New England embroideries of the late seventeenth through early nineteenth centuries constitute another strong area, as does the group of embroideries from Greece and the Greek islands. With the Elizabeth Day McCormick Collection the museum received its most important and extensive single collection of costumes and costume accessories. Gifts from other donors round out a superior collection of costume material dating from the sixteenth century to the present.

Most of the important tapestries hang in the Tapestry Gallery; others, as well as some of the textiles, are to be seen on exhibition in the galleries devoted to the decorative arts of Europe, America, and the Near East. Changing exhibitions of textiles from all parts of the collection are held in the two textile galleries, located on floor 1 of the museum. The remainder of the textile collection is kept in storage and may be consulted upon application in the Textile Study Room on floor 0.

EMBROIDERED BURIAL MANTLE. Polychrome wool yarns on wool cloth. Peruvian, Paracas culture, probably from Paracas Necropolis, possibly 300-200 B.C.   H. 47½ in., l. 96½ in. *Ross Collection. 16.34a*

Remarkable in design, execution, and function, this mantle is typical of the highly decorated textiles that formed part of the funerary bundles found on the Paracas peninsula of Peru. Worked by a professional embroiderer, this garment was intended to be used only as one of many layers of cloth to form a mummy bundle. Apparently, this mantle was needed for the funeral rite before it could be completed, as it was left unfinished.

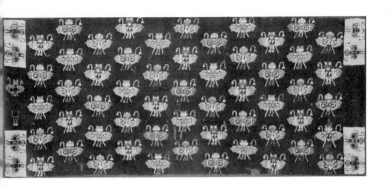

EMBROIDERED BURIAL MANTLE (detail). Polychrome wool yarns on wool cloth, Peruvian, Paracas culture, probably from Paracas Necropolis, possibly 300-200 B.C. H. 35⅜ in., l. 102¾ in. *Ross Collection. 16.31*

FRAGMENTS OF A CURTAIN (detail). Wool and linen tapestry. Eastern Mediterranean, probably 6th-7th century A.D.   H. 72½ in., w. 36½ in. *Charles Potter Kling Fund. 57.180*

Among the thousands of late antique textiles preserved in Egyptian burial grounds, few examples show large-scale figure compositions. Because of its unusual pictorial character and fine quality, these fragments of tapestry weaving are important in the history of art as an indication of some of the sources of early medieval styles.

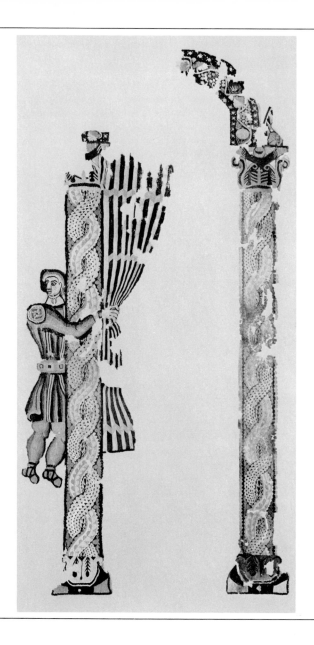

DETAIL OF A NECKLINE ORNAMENT. Silk, wool, and gold tapestry. Late
Hellenistic, probably 5th century A.D.   W. 6¼ in., l. 22⅜ in. *Charles Potter*
Kling Fund. 46.401
Drawing the line between painting and weaving in the late Hellenistic world
seems arbitrary and unnecessary when one examines this extraordinarily fine bit
of tapestry weaving. Executed in delicately tinted wools and sparkling gold
threads, this ornament once bordered the neck opening of a tunic or similar
garment and proves that some ancient costumes were far more splendid than
the bulk of surviving examples would suggest.

FRAGMENT OF THE SHROUD OF VIVENTIA. Silk weaving. Byzantine, 8th
century.   H. 8 in., w. 13¾ in. *1931 Purchase Fund. 33.648*
According to tradition this fragment of silk weaving was found in the tomb of
Viventia, daughter of Pepin the Short, in the Church of St. Ursula at Cologne.
The pattern may have inspired the fighting animals in roundels shown in the
famous European tapestry woven around 1000 A.D. and formerly preserved in the
Church of St. Gereon, also in Cologne.

FRAGMENT OF A SHROUD (detail). Silk weaving. Persian, Buyid Period, 11th
century.   H. 27½ in., w. 14 in. *William Francis Warden Fund. 50.3428*
This is one of a group of Buyid and Seluk period silks said to have been found
at a burial site near the city of Raiy in Persia. This example is of particularly
handsome design, unusual for the relatively large areas of plain color and for
the scale network. The inscription reads: "Order of the Emir Ghiyat al-umma
Diha al-milla Muhammad, son of Sa'id, son of Ali, al Harithi, may God
lengthen his life." The words "umma" and "milla" refer to geographical units
established by the Buyids.

MITRE. Near Eastern silk, embroidered in Germany. Salzburg, from the Church of St. Peter, early 13th century. H. 8⅜ in., w. 11 in. *Helen and Alice Colburn Fund. 38.887*
Mentioned in the oldest surviving inventory of the Benedictine abbey Church of St. Peter in Salzburg as one of "three old mitres," this piece shows the early thirteenth century form of the vestment with points lower than those of later times. The privilege of wearing a mitre, a headdress generally proper to bishops and granted only to certain abbots, was granted to the abbots of St. Peter's in 1231. This is an example of the *mitre auriphrygiata*, characterized by gold embroidery on white silk, which could be granted only to abbots exempt from the jurisdiction of a bishop.

CHASUBLE. Sicilian silk, with woven orphreys and embroidered inscription. Salzburg, from the Church of St. Peter, second half of the 12th century. Center back l. 60¼ in. *Ellen Frances Mason Fund. 33.676*
The inscription embroidered in Latin on the hem reads: "Heinrich, the sinner, completed this noble garment for St. Peter's altar, that it may be his helper." Possibly "Heinrich" was the Heinrich who was abbot of the monastery between 1167 and 1188. The gold orphreys are probably of Sicilian manufacture. The black ground cloth was made on Islamic looms of uncertain provenance. An Arabic inscription, "Great is God," is found under the orphreys. Probably owing to the presence of an inscription on the hem, this is one of the few surviving chasubles in the original twelfth century cone shape, which was not cut down when the fashion later changed to an abbreviated oblong shape.

FRAGMENT OF SILK WEAVING. Italian, Lucca, second half 14th century.
H. 20⅛ in., w. 24 in. *Arthur Mason Knapp Fund. 30.654*
Innovations in weaving and new freedom and liveliness in designing combined
in fourteenth century Italy to make possible the production of such vigorous
silk weavings as this one. The pattern, which shows Chinese influence, features
pairs of fantastic animals amid castles and a floral ground.

EMBROIDERED PANEL FROM AN ANTEPENDIUM. The Crucifixion. Polychrome
silk and gilt-silver yarns on cotton and linen fabric. Italian, Florence, late 14th
century.   H. 11¼in., w. 16½ in. *Helen and Alice Colburn Fund. 43.131*
Ecclesiastical embroidery was at its height in Italy in the fourteenth century, as
this lovely panel demonstrates. In drawing and execution it resembles those in a
large altar frontal signed "Geri Lapi richamatore me fecit in Florentia" in the
Collegiate Church of Maria de la Sec in Manresa near Barcelona, Spain.

WILD MEN, ANIMALS, AND MOORS (detail). Wool and linen tapestry. German,
Upper Rhine, late 14th-early 15th century.   H. 39⅜ in., l. 193 in. *Charles Potter
Kling Fund. 54.1431*
The scenes represented in this tapestry cannot yet be precisely interpreted, but
related tapestries in Europe appear to have some connection with popular love
themes. This tapestry shows exceptionally fine weaving and exquisite combinations of colors. The coats of arms shown on shields and helmets along the base
of the tapestry refer to the Blümel and Zorn families of Strasbourg.

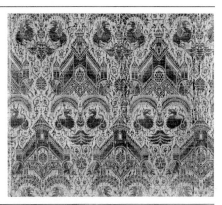

MITRE. Silk, silver, and gilt-silver yarns embroidered on silk, with pearls, glass, and gilt-metal trim. Italian, late 14th or early 15th century. H. 14¼ in., w. 12½ in. *Edward J. and Mary S. Holmes Fund. 1972.386*
The solidly embroidered front and back panels of this mitre have eight medallions each, arranged in an inverted T, in which are embroidered in polychrome silks figures of Christ, the Virgin, two bishops and twelve saints and prophets. Each panel also has two medallions, each of which contains an angel, again embroidered in polychrome silks.

MARTYRDOM OF ST. PAUL. Wool, silk, and metal thread tapestry. Franco-Flemish, ca. 1460. H. 109⅞ in., w. 80¼ in. *Francis Bartlett Fund. 38.758*
This tapestry is one of a series commissioned in 1460 by Guillaume de Hellande (Bishop of Beauvais, (1444-1462) for the Cathedral of Saint Peter at Beauvais. The shields in the upper left and lower right corners display the quartered arms of his father and mother, and those in the upper right and lower left corners display the arms of the Bishopric of Beauvais. The martyrdom, as depicted here, follows the account given in *The Golden Legend*. In the foreground an executioner has just severed St. Paul's head, which lies in the lower right corner of the tapestry. In the left background stand a group of pagans, with Nero at their center. A group of Christians stand in the right background. God the father appears in the sky to receive the saint's soul, represented as a nude infant. Tops of the buildings of Rome appear in the distance. The blossoming plants along the bottom edge of the tapestry are forerunners of those in the millefleurs tapestries. The inscription that appears in French at the top of the tapestry reads:

How Saint Paul was beheaded outside Rome.

His head, separated from the body, made three jumps.

A second inscription in Latin, to the left of the severed head, reads: "For me life is Christ and death is gain." The word "Peace" appears eight times around the periphery of the grouped figures.

FRAGMENT OF DOUBLE CLOTH (detail). Silk and silver yarns. Persian, Safavid, late 16th or early 17th century.   H. 6½ in., w. 5¾ in. *H. E. Bolles Fund. 39.296*
Intricately patterned double cloths achieved a technical and artistic high point in Persia under Safavid rule. This textile, which is completely reversible, shows groups of men in boats with ducks and fish swimming in the surrounding water. The design shows Chinese influence, especially in the drawing of the figures.

SCENES FROM THE PASSION OF CHRIST (detail). Wool and silk tapestry. Franco-Flemish, late 15th century.   H. 203¾ in., l. 350¾ in. *Gift of Robert Treat Paine II in memory of his son, Walter Cabot Paine. 29.1046*
Because of the superlative quality of its design and weaving and its excellent state of preservation, this is one of the most important tapestries to have survived from the golden age of tapestry weaving in Europe. The designer and weavers pressed the limitations of their craft to the utmost to present the story of the Passion with all the poignancy a panel painter could have hoped to express. During the first four centuries of its existence, the tapestry hung in the chapel at Knole, in Kent, England.

WOOL CARPET. Spanish, 15th century.   W. 79 in., l. 182¼ in. *Purchased in memory of Sarah Gore Flint Townsend. 39.614*
The design of geometric interlacings and small medallions placed on the field o this Spanish carpet is very similar to that of Turkish carpets. Patterns similar to this are frequently called "Holbein," as they appear in some of the paintings of this artist.

NARCISSUS. Wool and silk tapestry. French or Franco-Flemish, late 15th or early 16th century.   H. 111 in., w. 122½ in. *Charles Potter Kling Fund. 68.114*
The handsome Narcissus bends over a fountain to study his reflection in its pool. He wears a plumed headdress, a cape that flows out behind him, an elaborately woven doublet, and hose with his name woven into the left leg. Various birds and animals dot the field around the fountain. This is among the greatest *millefleurs* or "thousand flowers" tapestries, named for the floral plants that form the background.

ORPHEUS (detail). Linen damask weaving. Possibly Dutch, ca. 1650.   H. 41½ in.,
w. 29⅛ in. *Arthur Tracy Cabot Fund. 65.152*
This is one of a large group of European damask napkins in the museum's
collection. Its subject is Orpheus, seated under a tree playing his lyre, with
various animals gathered around him.

ABRAHAM'S SACRIFICE OF ISAAC. Wool, silk, and linen tapestry. German, possibly Wolfenbüttel, ca. 1600. H. 98¾ in., w. 73⅝ in. *Gift of Mrs. Alfred M. Tozzer. 64.41*

The bold design of this German tapestry shows scenes from the sacrifice of Isaac. Figures of six virtues (Patience, Prudence, Charity, Courage, Hope, and Faith) are placed in the border between bouquets of fruits and flowers.

WOMAN'S WAISTCOAT AND MATCHING COIF. Silver and gilt-silver yarns, lace and spangles, on undyed linen fabric (collar and skirt reconstructed). English, late 16th century. Back l. 19½ in. *The Elizabeth Day McCormick Collection. 43.243, 43.244a*
According to family tradition Queen Elizabeth I left this waistcoat and coif as a gift for the wife of Roger Woodhouse when she visited their house, Kimberley, in Norfolk, on August 22, 1578. It is one of the richest sets of garments to have survived from a brilliant period in the history of English art.

HUNTING CARPET (details). Silk, silver, and gilt-silver yarns. Persian, 1525-1550. L. 189 in., w. 100⅜ in. *Gift of John Goelet, Centennial Purchase Fund, and restricted funds. 66.293*
One of the masterpieces of Persian art produced during the reign of Shah Tahmasp, this carpet is one of four hunting carpets of world renown. The ground fabric and pile are made entirely of silk yarns, and the carpet has approximately 800 knots per square inch. In addition, silk yarns wrapped with flat silver or gilt-silver wires have been brocaded into the ground fabric in many places to represent the pools of water or objects made of metal. It is believed that the carpet was woven in a court manufactory, probably at Kashan in Central Persia. Surrounded by curling vine tendrils with exotic blossoms, mounted riders attack game beasts in the carpet's field. An endless garden fills the border with trees, flowering plants, and pools of water, before which sumptuously dressed men take their ease.

PART OF A BORDER (detail). Bobbin lace. Probably Italian, late 16th-early 17th century.   W. 6⅝ in., l. 106⅝ in. *Bequest of J. W. Paige. 95.955*
Created with an airy openness, this border was worked with bobbins on a pillow. Men, women, and crested birds fill the compartments.

WOOL CARPET. *Landscape with Figures and Mythological Beasts.* Indian, Mughal, early 17th century.   W. 41½ in., l. 95⅝ in. *Gift in the name of Frederick L. Ames. 93.1480*
With good reason this is one of the most admired and most published of all oriental carpets. Combining some of the finest qualities of miniature paintings with the best traditional carpet motifs and workmanship, the designer and weavers produced a major monument in the history of Mughal art.

COVER. Embroidered linen, with reticello bands and border. English, early 17th century.   W. 33⅞ in., l. 37¾ in. *Gift of Philip Lehman in memory of his wife, Carrie L. Lehman. 38.1082*
The Elizabethan Age was one of the great periods in English embroidery. The floral scroll pattern seen here was typical. The early seventeenth century also marks a very early and high point in the development of the needle lace technique in Italy. The combination of the two techniques is unusual, but the circular elements of both harmonize well.

COVER. Cut and uncut silk velvet with gilt-silver wires. Probably Italian, late 17th century.   H. 25 in., w. 51¼ in. *Anonymous gift. 65.597*
A Palladian-style façade is shown in this tour de force of weaving. Velvets with pictorial subject matter are unusual in this period. The cut and uncut pile here gives a three-dimensional effect. At one time the entire background was woven with gilt-silver wires, which were apparently deliberately removed at some time after the weaving was completed.

SCENES FROM GENESIS (detail). *Joseph Sold by His Brothers.* Wool, linen, silk, and metal thread tapestry. Southern Denmark, 17th century.   H. 24½ in., l. 201 in. *Charles Potter Kling Fund. 62.1012*
The figure compositions of this tapestry are derived from a series of woodcuts by Virgil Solis of Nuremberg. They show the sacrifice of Isaac, Jacob's dream, Jacob showing straked rods to Laban's flocks, Jacob wrestling with the angel, Joseph being raised from the pit and Joseph sold by his brothers, Joseph escaping from Potiphar's wife, and Joseph explaining Pharaoh's dream. This tapestry was probably used as a valance running around the top of a bed or perhaps to line the wall above a row of benches or choirstalls.

FRAGMENT OF A LACE BORDER (detail). Darned netting. Italian, 17th century. W. 11 in., l. 29⅛ in. *Gift of Henry W. Bliss. 23.642*
The exuberant design of this lace fragment shows a man and birds making their way through a crowded floral border. The technique employed here, that of building a design on an open net ground, is one of the most popular ones in lacemaking.

BED FURNISHINGS. Wool embroidery on cotton and linen. English, 1725-1750. H. 85 in. *J. H. and E. A. Payne Fund. 63.1023-63.1029*
Richly embroidered bed hangings with large foliage and floral motifs were popular in England around 1700. Bizarre flowers, exotic fruits, and leaves extend from two different kinds of trees, worked in yellow and red yarns with touches of orange and brown. The pattern is similar to that of laces, various silk weavings, and Indian painted cottons of the late seventeenth and early eighteenth centuries. Many such sets were embroidered in the home, but these hangings were surely worked by a professional. The set includes seven matching chair seat covers.

COVER FOR A CHAIR BACK OR CUSHION. Silk and cotton tapestry. Peruvian, colonial period, probably 17th century. H. 17⅞ in., w. 16¾ in. *Charles Potter Kling Fund. 60.794*
Highly skilled tapestry weaving was done by the Peruvian natives for centuries before the Spanish conquest. However, the invasion of the Spaniards brought changes in the designs of these textiles. Here a shield of arms, surmounted by a plumed helmet and an armoured arm with sword in fist, is centered in an elaborate framework of flowers, fruits, birds, and animals. The use of silk here is highly unusual and occurs in Peruvian textiles only after the conquest.

FEATHERWORK PANEL. Peruvian, ca. A.D. 1200-1400. H. 50 in., w. 37½ in. *Arthur Tracy Cabot Fund. 1971.76*
The feathers in this panel are all natural colors. Each one is applied by embroidery onto a cotton ground to create the overall design.

EMBROIDERED BOX. Silks and metal threads in flat and raised work; wax effigy inside cover. English, second half 17th century. H. 14 in., w. 10 in., l. 12⅝ in. *Gift of Mrs. Elizabeth Learned Peabody. 59.1033*
This jewelry casket has the story of Isaac and Rebecca (Genesis 24) as the main theme of its embroidery, with other Old Testament scenes as well as various birds, animals, insects, and flowers filling the remaining surfaces. The raised work figures clothed in needlework have faces and hands of finely carved wood. The superb quality of workmanship suggests that the casket was made by professional craftsmen.

COVER. Cotton, painted and treated with mordants, resist medium, and dyes. Indian (Golconda?), 1630-1700. H. 26⅜ in., w. 32¼ in. *Gift of John Goelet. 66.230*
The field shows *peris*, mythical beings, dancing and playing instruments. Gazelle-like animals lie among the rocks in the lower left corner, and appear elsewhere in the field, with birds, hares, plants, and trees. The border shows an arabesque of polychrome leaves and medallions.

WOVEN SHAWL (detail). Kashmir, late 17th-early 18th century. W. 49¾ in., l. 93¼ in. *Anonymous gift, in the name of Mrs. Arthur T. Cabot. 45.540*
So rich and glossy is the substance of this fabric that it is hard to believe the threads are of wool rather than silk. The soft, glistening yarns, incredibly fine, were spun from the fleece of a species of the mountain goat. The superior quality of the fabric and the character of the pattern indicate that this shawl was woven at a very early date, a period from which only a few other examples have survived.

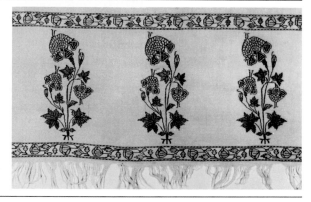

PETTICOAT BORDER (detail). Crewels embroidered on linen. New England, 1725-1750. H. 8¼ in., w. 75 in. *John Wheelock Elliot Fund. 25.186a*
New England schoolgirls learned to embroider by working samplers, canvas-work pictures, and petticoat borders. The motifs used here recur frequently on other embroidered borders, pictures, and chair seat covers and were probably provided by the young girl's instructress.

DRESS termed *Robe Battante*. Silk lampas. French, second quarter 18th century. *The Elizabeth Day McCormick Collection. 43.664*
Although the sumptuous silk used in this dress suggests that it was intended for some grand occasion, contemporary portraits and prints indicate that dresses cut like this were worn informally at home. This dress shows the characteristic cut of the *robe battante* (literally, "swinging dress," from the movement of its billowing looseness). The skirt and matching petticoat, worn over hoops or *paniers,* are voluminous and loose, the skirt melting imperceptibly into a loose-fitting bodice. This suppression of the waistline has been emphasized by carrying the deep, flat pleats of the back (so-called Watteau pleats) up over the shoulders and straight down either side of the overdress, which hangs open in front. Except for its shoulder area, the dress is quite independent of the shape of the body beneath.

DETAIL OF AN EMBROIDERED BED COVER. Polychrome silks on linen. Greek Islands, Skyros, 18th century.   W. 63½ in., l. 96½ in. *Gift in the name of Abby L. Tyler. 33.23*
Typical of the embroideries attributed to Skyros, this bed cover features roosters and other birds, flowers, and small human figures in its pattern. Both bright, cheerful colors and softer pastels have been used, and the design is at once lively and refined.

THE LUNCHEON, from *La Noble Pastorale*. Designed by François Boucher. Wool and silk tapestry. French, Beauvais, dated 1756.   H. 13⅛ in., w. 133¼ in. *Francis Bartlett Fund. 40.66*
A number of French eighteenth century tapestry series were based on designs provided by the French painter François Boucher. This tapestry, from the series "La Noble Pastorale" or "Les Beaux Pastorales," celebrates the simple pleasures of bucolic life as it was romantically envisaged by the fashionable world in France in the eighteenth century. The armorial cartouche in the center of the upper border shows the arms of France and Navarre surmounted by the royal crown and encircled by the collars of the orders of St. Michael and of the Holy Spirit. These are the arms of France as borne by Louis XV.

THE VOLUNTEER FURNITURE: LORD CHARLEMONT AT THE PROVINCIAL REVIEW, PHOENIX PARK, DUBLIN, 1782 (detail). Copperplate and woodblock printed and hand painted on linen and cotton. Irish, Leixlip, printed by Thomas Harpur, 1783. *Gift of Mrs. Jason Westerfield. 58.1177*
When the English withdrew troops from Ireland to use in the American war, the Irish, fearing an invasion from France, organized corps of volunteers. James Caulfield, Earl of Charlemont, was their commander-in-chief. The design of the chintz is not merely commemorative, however, but has a coherent decorative scheme as well. It is also technically one of the most elaborate chintzes made in Europe up to that time.

EMBROIDERED COAT OF ARMS. Silk and metal threads, on satin. New England, Connecticut, third quarter 18th century.   H. 26 in., w. 25½ in. *Gift of Miss Ella Winthrop Saltonstall in memory of Francis G. Saltonstall. 43.75*

WOOL BROCADED WEAVING (detail). English, London or Norwich, 1750-1775. L. 35 in., w. 18 in. *Special Textile Fund. 61.148*

FRAGMENT OF PRINTED COTTON. French, Nantes, late 18th century.   H. 16⅜ in., w. 21⅜ in. *Textile Income Purchase Fund. 55.102*
The exquisite color printing in this textile, extremely difficult to achieve at the time it was done, proves that technological progress in industry was relatively rapid long before our own time. The grace and delicacy of the pattern and colors set this textile in a prominent place in the history of fine textile printing.

PIECE OF SILK DAMASK. French, first half 19th century. W. 21 in., l. 27⅛ in.
Gift of David M. K. McKibbon. 56.328
This damask woven with a bee, an emblem of Napoleon I, is part of a set of
hangings taken to England early in the nineteenth century by Lord Stuart de
Rothesay. It is believed to have been woven for the Château of Malmaison.

DETAIL OF A SATIN WALL PANEL. Brocaded and embroidered silk. French,
Lyons, late 18th century. H. 140 in., w. 24 in. *Arthur Mason Knapp Fund. 57.746*
This is one of several panels from a set of woven wall hangings intended for use
in the Royal Palace at Madrid. The design for this project is said to have been
made by Jean-Démosthène Dugourc, the official festival, interior, and theater
designer to the French court. In this instance Dugourc was commissioned by the
firm of Camille Pernon et Cie. of Lyons, which regularly provided special textiles
for the use of the Spanish court.